# LEEDS METROPOLITAN UNIVERSITY

## City Campus Learning Centre
## Leeds LS1 3HE

Items should be returned on or before the last date shown below
All items are subject to recall if required by another reader.

Charges are levied for the late return of items.

Renewal may be made by personal application, in writing or by telephoning
(0113) 283 3106 and quoting the barcode number below.

| Date Due | Date Due | Date Due | Date Due |
|----------|----------|----------|----------|
|          |          |          |          |

3308a

FRONTISPIECE.   PLATE 1.   Last Judgement   [No. 49]

# THE BOOK OF HOURS

## OF

# CATHERINE OF CLEVES

by John Plummer

*Foreword by Frederick B. Adams, Jr.,*
*incorporating comments by*
*Harry Bober, L. M. J. Delaissé, Millard Meiss,*
*and Erwin Panofsky*

NEW YORK

THE PIERPONT MORGAN LIBRARY

1964

COPYRIGHT © 1964

BY THE PIERPONT MORGAN LIBRARY

PRINTED IN THE UNITED STATES OF AMERICA

# CONTENTS

# FOREWORD

This publication is a preliminary report on the complete Book of Hours of Catherine of Cleves, a manuscript compilation of Latin prayers for private devotions, written on vellum and illuminated by an unidentified artist of Utrecht, probably in the years around 1435, and preserved in almost immaculate condition.

The beauty and originality of this finest of Dutch manuscripts have not been adequately recognized in modern times, because no more than a portion of it has hitherto been publicly known. The Morgan Library therefore counts it a rare privilege to be able to exhibit the entire manuscript and to publish this description of it, in the expectation that the Master of the Cleves Hours will finally be recognized as a major artist of the fifteenth century, who has displayed the full range of his artistic skill and intellectual powers in this single work, his masterpiece.

Early in the present century, the Duke of Arenberg lent for exhibition in Düsseldorf a remarkable Dutch *Horae* which had been made for Catherine of Cleves, Duchess of Guelders, and several inadequate illustrations of its miniatures were published. Few were privileged to see the manuscript itself until several years ago, when the present Duke of Arenberg decided to sell the book, and it was acquired for the Guennol Collection through Mr. H. P. Kraus. The new owner generously lent it to the exhibition of Dutch mediaeval art organized by the Rijksmuseum in Amsterdam in 1958, where its merits became better known. Down through the years, the Arenberg manuscript has always been considered as complete, and some scholars have even described it as having a calendar, which is its one conspicuous deficiency.

In the spring of 1963, a New York art dealer received several manuscripts on consignment from a private owner in Europe. I had the good fortune to be the first person invited to examine them. It would be difficult to describe the mounting excitement with which I turned the leaves of one, which I took to be another Book of Hours of the highest quality from the hand of the artist then variously known as the Arenberg Master or the Master of Catherine of Cleves. With the strong support of the Library's president, Mr. Henry S. Morgan, I immediately initiated the course of events which led to our acquisition of the manuscript, now designated as M.917, a purchase made possible by the enthusiasm and great generosity of our Fellows.

Ten weeks later, thinking that an instructive comparison might be made between the Guennol Collection's manuscript and ours, we asked the owner if he would lend it to us for this purpose, and he promptly did so. When the two volumes were examined side by side, and it was recognized that both were incomplete, their apparently complementary character suggested the strong probability that they were parts of a whole whose true significance might only now begin to be appreciated.

During May of 1964, Dr. John Plummer, the Library's Curator of Mediaeval and Renaissance Manuscripts, toured European libraries to examine manuscripts attributed to the Cleves Master. He has dedicated the ensuing summer to a study of the two portions of the Cleves Hours, and his painstaking reconstruction of the original sequence of the leaves, achieved by iconographic, textual, and physical analysis, has proved beyond any doubt that they once formed a single rationally organized Book of Hours. The 157 surviving miniatures, out of a possible maximum originally of 166, could now be rearranged in proper order. They are so presented in our exhibition by means of color transparencies photographed in actual size, and are so described in this booklet.

Although a number of manuscripts can be attributed to the Master of the Cleves Hours or his workshop, this one contains many times the number of miniatures found in any other manuscript by him, and here the miniatures and the principal border decorations are by his hand alone. This is uncommon, to say the least, in so elaborate a manuscript. The task must have occupied the illuminator for several years, and this hypothetical time span is corroborated by the evidence of his increasing artistic independence from established formulas. Whereas most ambitious manuscripts show a progressive decline in imaginative vigor, the opposite is true of the Cleves Hours. In general, the earlier miniatures and borders still reflect acquaintance with older and contemporary illuminations and panel paintings, but the later ones freely develop themes and details which seem to have no specific antecedents. Indeed, there still remain a few elements of the artist's iconography which we do not fully understand, and the same applies to the relationship of the borders to the miniatures.

As the contributors to this Foreword demonstrate below, every art historian and connoisseur will form his own estimate of the excellence and individuality of the Master of the Cleves Hours, of the dating of his masterpiece, of his worldly attitudes and liturgical knowledge, and of the place to which he must now be assigned in Northern art from the fifteenth century onward. Knowing him is a slow process, and the wonder grows with improved acquaintance.

He was a man who took obvious delight in his surroundings, and he shows us a number of homely occupations, among them milking a cow, churning butter, keeping a market stall, hunting with dogs, dressing fowl, snaring birds, sheep-shearing, selling wine at a stand, and baking bread. He finds beauty in the works of nature, such as butterflies, vegetables, flowers, fruit, mussels, birds, and fish; but he is seemingly more impressed by man-made beauty, in tiles, textiles, furniture, jewelry, and buildings.

Despite his attention to everyday things, which he never treats half-heartedly or mechanically, he is not a plebeian painter. He prefers the courtly world, with its luxurious appointments and richly dressed nobles; the buildings in his colorful landscape backgrounds are chiefly castles, with only an occasional walled town or windmill. Even his Holy Family at home wears rusticity with unmistakable elegance, and the stable in which Christ is visited by the Magi is charmingly eccentric rather than rude. The saints, despite the symbols of their martyrdom, are imperturbable lords and ladies, and the stag which appears to St. Hubert is so well-bred that he crosses his forelegs in the presence of the miracle.

This auspicious and aristocratic atmosphere is eminently appropriate for the prayer-book of a young duchess of distinguished ancestry and considerable wealth. The ancient town of Cleves was the seat of the counts of Cleves as early as the eleventh century, and their castle of Schwanenburg, with its impressive Schwanenturm, is associated with the mediaeval legend of the Knight of the

Swan, familiar to operagoers from Wagner's *Lohengrin*. Cleves was made a duchy in 1417, the year of Catherine's birth. It is not surprising to find, in a manuscript probably commissioned for her by her father, an array of coats of arms that emphasizes the importance of her forebears. This is, in fact, only the beginning of a pictorial program intended to serve at one level as a constant reminder to Catherine of her special privileges and obligations. Her duties to the poor and crippled are implied in more than one miniature, and especially in that of Piety, the sixth gift of the Holy Ghost, depicted as a lady distributing alms. Her devotional duties to God and the Holy Family are emphasized in the scene which shows her kneeling before the crucifix (where God indicates that He will take a personal interest in her salvation), and in the use of her elaborate rosary to form a border around the miniature of the Adoration of the Magi. On the other hand, Catherine's marital obligations are minimized, and there are only three apparent references to her husband, Duke Arnold of nearby Guelders, whose wealth and power matched those of Cleves. The gentleman praying to Christ in the miniature of Fear of the Lord, the seventh gift of the Holy Ghost, probably represents Duke Arnold; his device is of course incorporated in Catherine's coat of arms in the first miniature; and some of his coinage occurs in one of the borders—but otherwise he is ignored. History records that Catherine was violent and ambitious and that, some thirty years after her marriage, she joined her son in a conspiracy against her husband.

Four art historians, who have had some opportunity to become acquainted with the separate parts of the manuscript, were invited to contribute their observations for publication here. Professor Bober has made a careful study of the Arenberg-Guennol manuscript, and we are indebted to him for valuable suggestions and bibliographical information. With this exception, the comments which follow are not based on intensive research; indeed, until the opening of the exhibition, detailed examination of the reconstituted Cleves Hours was not possible for anybody outside the staff of the Morgan Library. We are grateful to the authors for their exceedingly helpful observations, and their willingness to make them under these conditions.

[ 4 ]

## Harry Bober

The tale of the Book of Hours written and illuminated for
Catherine of Cleves and now the remarkable object of this historic
exhibition, began simply enough. It was undertaken as a wedding
present for Catherine and completed within the year after January
26, 1430, the date of her marriage to Arnold, Duke of Guelders.
Against this and further clear documentation for the beginning
lies the complete obscurity of four subsequent centuries when we
hear nothing of the manuscript. As for studies of the manuscript
during the hundred years since it began to be noticed just after the
middle of the nineteenth century, these yielded abundant enlight-
enment but also, as we can only now recognize, an abundant
admixture of paradox.

The elements of the paradox are manifold. While frequently
and rightly acclaimed as just about the most famous single work
of northern Netherlandish illumination, it is probable that no
scholar ever even saw the manuscript between 1904 (when it was
exhibited at Düsseldorf) and 1958 (when it was acquired for the
Guennol Collection in New York from the library of the Duke of
Arenberg). As for those rare few who had seen it, they could not
have seen the manuscript which was presented to Catherine—what
they saw was approximately half of that manuscript. Only now,
since the Pierpont Morgan Library acquired its manuscript and
has been able to examine it, do we know for certain that the
Guennol and Morgan manuscripts comprise complementary portions of the same original work. In the mid-nineteenth century the
Hours of Catherine of Cleves was skillfully divided into two independent volumes. Such was the elaboration of its liturgical con-
tent and the wealth of its illumination that nobody even suspected
that the Arenberg manuscript (which has always been designated
as *the* Hours of Catherine of Cleves) was, for all its magnificence,
only about half of the unimaginably magnificent whole.

The partition of the manuscript, with mysterious loss from sight
of the Morgan portion, and the inaccessibility of the Arenberg
(Guennol) portion, were the main factors in the prevalently super-
ficial, even if enthusiastic, appraisal of the master who executed

its miniatures. Known largely from poor photographs of some few of the Arenberg miniatures, and even poorer reproductions in books, there was but the merest intuition of the art of this miniaturist, dubbed alternatively the "Arenberg Master" or the "Master of Catherine of Cleves." After somewhat vague incantations of his important standing, discussions of his art turned quickly to the same few miniatures known to relate to panel paintings by the Master of Flémalle and Jan van Eyck.

Even this circumscribed view of his art was not developed to its full extent, for the complete manuscript not only shows further links to the brothers van Eyck, but also entirely new evidence for the Rohan Master. Indeed, familiarity with the actual miniatures shows that the essential quality of the master's art has been overlooked, even in this sphere, at the expense of emphasizing their sources in panel painting. The Cleves Master was an acute observer, alert to the most advanced developments in contemporary painting but, above all, a miniaturist in the best sense of the tradition. Under his brush, sources were transformed and completely assimilated to a brilliant mode of miniature painting.

It seems hardly to have been noticed, even though the evidence was present in the Arenberg manuscript alone, that the "derivative" compositions are but a small minority in his formidable miniature *oeuvre*. His miniatures are not to be seen as southern Netherlandish works, whose surface stillness and finish were so esteemed in the later nineteenth-century esthetic. The Cleves Master is distinctively and superlatively northern Netherlandish with that more tart taste and bite that is apt to be better understood in our day. His brushwork tends to be dynamic and even violent, his color tonalities more piercing, even strident, than what is to be seen in Flemish art. He is, in this Book of Hours, the *summa* of his art, the northern Netherlandish miniaturist *par excellence*.

This sketch can only suggest something of the individuality of the Master of the Hours of Catherine of Cleves and evoke some of the aspects which make the Guennol-Morgan manuscript his masterwork. It can scarcely touch upon his almost cinematographic compositional sequences and inventions, his limitless imaginative and thematic resources in marginal scenes and vignettes, and his iconographic virtuosity.

Time, circumstances, and the devotion of manuscript lovers have conspired to be very good to us in preserving both portions of this great manuscript—even to the extent of bringing them together in this country and city, albeit in two independent collections.

## L. M. J. Delaissé

It is immediately obvious that the Hours of Catherine of Cleves is a most attractive manuscript, and closer study confirms that, by the nature and the style of its decoration and illustration, it is the best production of the Dutch school, and furthermore a key to the understanding of later panel painting in Holland.

Around 1400 and during the following decades Western Europe produced many exceptional manuscripts, which showed a great innovation in iconographical themes and an unexpected variety of styles rendered more complex by the movement of artists from country to country. Even against this competition the Cleves Hours is a choice piece, not only of the Dutch school, but in the whole production of the first half of the fifteenth century.

No other manuscript showed so early such a wealth of knowledge of, and feeling for, the external world and everyday human activity as the Cleves Hours; its marginal decoration and its miniatures depict for us the less important attributes of living as well as the complex reactions of the human soul. No other miniaturist manifested before 1450 such a straightforward and spontaneous vision and rendering of objective reality; or such an understanding of, and love for, life in its broadest sense, with no need for escapist idealisation.

Is it necessary to stress that the style of the miniatures, so original for the time, announces seventeenth-century painting in Holland? Those homely scenes (for instance the representation of the Holy Family at two successive moments of Jesus's childhood, or of illness, death, and afterdeath), and the still life studies in the borders of the manuscript, could be found in later Dutch panels. Such a

[ 7 ]

continuity gives more weight and significance to the stylistic originality of the miniatures.

This human flavor, so typically Dutch, is also present in many contemporary Dutch manuscripts, such as the Morgan Library's Egmond Breviary, M.87, but never in such a concentrated and almost ostentatious manner. I was therefore delighted when I learned of the Library's acquisition of an unrecorded portion of the Cleves Hours, and was allowed to add this incomparable material as a postscript to my forthcoming book on Dutch manuscript illumination. No other manuscript could better help us to observe and appreciate the originality of Dutch art already before the middle of the fifteenth century.

The Hours of Catherine of Cleves is also unique for another reason. After pages and pages of conscientious and high quality work, we suddenly see the miniaturist letting his imagination run free and producing the most unusual series of miniatures and marginal decorations that is known. This exciting experience of an artist in the full tide of his creative power is certainly a major attraction of this exceptional manuscript.

## Millard Meiss

Art is always full of surprises, and the Master of the Hours of Catherine of Cleves offers us a stirring one. Right in the heyday of one of the great movements in Western painting he inspected its products, chose what he wanted or had to have for his patrons, and then went his own way. He demonstrates that he could create masterpieces in the style of the great panel painters—his tree growing from the grave of Adam seems just that, though I cannot think of any panel painting in which a single object is set, alone, in a landscape that rolls back to the sky, or in which this vast space has so much *Stimmung*. Of course, working in small scale and on a less smooth surface than gessoed panel he was bound to reduce the marvellous subtleties of Eyck and Flémalle, but he compensated for this simpler style in two chief respects. He could paint subjects and motifs not suitable for the more formal and more monumental mode of panel painting. Belonging to the Dutch tradition, he inclined especially toward homely subjects, such as the Holy Family *chez eux,* the Virgin (really a Madonna of Humility) seated on or close to the floor nursing her Child while Joseph, relatively enthroned on a rustic chair, solemnly spoons gruel from a bowl. The illuminator tells the story of the Cross as if it had happened yesterday on the Maas, with the Queen of Sheba, wading through the water, holding up her skirt to keep it dry. In this state she is first greeted by King Solomon—our master is really Piero della Francesca in reverse.

When transferring the new realism to the pages of a book our master saw fit to modify it, partly for purposes of adaptation and also to suit his own wish for a livelier, more agitated art. Thus he partly denied the vivid space of his interiors by the size and salience of the tiles in the floors, seeking by this and other means to maintain the older relationship between the miniature and the ornamented and inscribed folio. But it is in the borders that he broke most decisively with his cooler, nobler predecessors in panel painting. He often employed large patches of strident colors that seem to shout down subtler relations within the miniatures. Taking a cue from earlier illumination he filled many borders with "still-life." Never before however had the objects been repeated to form a kind of chain, and seldom were they rendered on so large a scale. One almost has the impression of seeing the borders through a magnifying glass while looking at the miniatures with binoculars. Such a juxtaposition introduces an astonishing element of fantasy into the new realism. Indeed the combination of subjects—St. Bartholomew surrounded by large pretzels, St. Lawrence by eels and fish, St. Ambrose by mussels—is nothing less than grotesque. Though I dare not interpret our master's intention, he seems to possess some of that late mediaeval sardonic humor that we know best in another, later painter from the same region, Hieronymus Bosch.

The acquisition of the unrecorded volume of the manuscript by the Morgan Library gives historians of art in the United States one more reason to be grateful to this unique institution.

## Erwin Panofsky

The manuscript is an acquisition which, even by the standards of the Morgan Library, must be considered a historic event. Quite apart from the fact that it represents the missing portion of a world-famous Book of Hours never suspected of being only half a manuscript, it profoundly changes our—or at least my—ideas about its illustrator, the Master of Catherine of Cleves. It remains true (witness, among other manuscripts, the Morgan Library's Egmond Breviary, M.87), that this Master absorbed the influence of the great new panel painters, Robert Campin and the van Eyck brothers, to such an extent that some of their lost compositions can be reconstructed with the aid of his miniatures. But the new acquisition has convinced me that I overestimated [in *Early Netherlandish Painting,* 1953] this imitative facet of his artistic personality and underestimated, or overlooked, both his indebtedness to the earlier French book illuminators (the Boucicaut Master, the Bedford Master, and the Rohan Master) and that amazing originality which shines forth in his marginal decorations.

I wonder, however, whether these admirable borders, entirely composed of large-scale and seemingly tangible objects, some homely, some edible, others precious, such as pearls, coins, medals, bird cages, textiles, butterflies, feathers, pretzels, mussels, trout, and eels,—whether these may not reflect the Master's active response as opposed to his passive surrender to the influence of the new panel painting? So far as I know, there is no real precedent for this pictorial "existentialism" in earlier marginal ornament. There we may find an occasional intrusion of such naturalistic still-life features, mostly on a very reduced scale, as Pucelle's insects, Jacquemart de Hesdin's birds, the Boucicaut Master's peacocks, or the Limbourg brothers' iris; but not a total displacement of the decorative by the representational, even illusionistic element. Could it be that the Master of Catherine of Cleves discovered that the margins of a manuscript page offered him a chance to employ the *ars nova* of the great panel painters for the large-scale and life-like presentation of small objects (thereby initiating an entirely novel type of border ornament), while in his narrative

[ 10 ]

miniatures he could provide only reduced and much abbreviated variations on their *invenzioni?* I leave it to *color che sanno* to decide whether this idea should be discarded as a flight of fancy or may be worth musing about.

♪♫♪♫

A clue supplied by Professor Bober led us to an examination of the *Bulletin du Bibliophile, douzième série,* Paris, 1856. Here we found a detailed description by the bookseller, Jacques Joseph Techener, of the Guennol volume in exactly the form in which it survives today, and a notice that it could be purchased for 15,000 francs. Even before this discovery, we had concluded—on the evidence of the binding of our portion of the manuscript, which was executed by Belz-Niedrée in the 1850's and gilt-tooled in the retrospective sixteenth-century style so much in vogue in France at the time of Napoleon III—that the manuscript was divided into two approximately equal parts some 110 years ago, by a clever but unscrupulous dealer into whose hands it had the misfortune to fall. The Niedrée binding is titled on the spine, *Heures de Catherine de Clèves/Martyrologe,* yet there are no clues in this Morgan volume sufficiently strong to point to the duchess as its original owner, although her appearance in several miniatures and the occasional use of her initials provide corroborative evidence once her ownership is known. On the other hand, the Guennol volume, which is in a nineteenth-century binding without spine titling, was unmistakably made for Catherine, since it contains her coat of arms and those of her eight great-great-grandfathers. Whoever specified the titling on the Niedrée binding could not have identified the manuscript as Catherine's if the relationship to it of the Guennol portion were not well known to him. By dividing his treasure, so deceptively as to make each part seem virtually complete, somebody was able to reap a double profit for his pains. Whether the offender was Techener himself is impossible to prove, but it is instructive to learn from Techener's own publications that one of his customers was an ancestor of the last private owner of the Morgan volume.

We cannot sufficiently express our thanks to the owner of the Guennol Collection for enabling us to reunite the two parts temporarily in our exhibition, for permitting us to photograph all his miniatures in color and a selection in black and white, and for allowing us to describe and illustrate his manuscript in its proper relationship to ours in this preliminary report on the Cleves Hours.

FREDERICK B. ADAMS, JR.

*August 31, 1964*

PLATE 2.  Holy Family at Supper  [No. 93]

# THE CLEVES HOURS AND ITS MASTER

From the first known mention of the manuscript, published by the dealer Jacques Joseph Techener in 1856, at which time he was offering it for sale at 15,000 francs, the Book of Hours made in Utrecht about 1435 for Catherine of Cleves has been regarded as the single volume that passed into the collections of the Dukes of Arenberg sometime before 1896, and into the Guennol Collection in 1958. This volume, though often discussed and reproduced in the last sixty years, has been examined by only a few scholars. For this reason, the descriptions of its contents have usually been incomplete, vague, and inaccurate. It has been frequently said, for example, that it has a calendar, which has even been described as being for use in the diocese of Utrecht, but the volume has no calendar. However, since some scholars did see it, there must be other reasons why its incompleteness was never recognized. First, the volume gives the impression of completeness; it is of a normal size for a Book of Hours, and has more miniatures than is usual for such a book. Second, it has the one essential text for a *Horae*, the Little Office of the Blessed Virgin, and several of the more or less normal texts, such as the Penitential Psalms, Litanies, Office of the Dead, and the Hours of the Cross, though not all are complete; of the normal components it lacks only the calendar and the Suffrages. Third, the contents of Books of Hours, both texts and pictures, vary widely, since a book of this kind was used primarily for private devotions and was not controlled by rigid liturgical requirements. And one final reason, the students of the volume were interested in the miniatures, whereas the text, which is of no historical importance, contains the only clear evidence of the volume's incompleteness.

Thus, when the Morgan volume arrived at the Library, there was no reason to connect it directly with the Arenberg-Guennol volume, other than the puzzling title on the spine, *Heures de Catherine de Clèves/Martyrologe*, although both were certainly by the same artist. The new volume was obviously not a Book of Hours, since it lacked the one essential text, the Little Office. At first glance it was thought to be a book of miscellaneous prayers, and it only became clear some time later, after the texts of the book were identified, especially those on each of the chaotically disarranged leaves in the first part, that the Morgan volume was incomplete, and that some of its texts were fragmentary. Its contents included a calendar, the Mass for the Dead, the Tuesday Hours of the Holy Ghost, part of the Wednesday Hours of All Saints, the Friday Hours of the Compassion of God *(Misericordia Dei)* and the Mass of the Cross, the Sabbath Hours and Mass of the Virgin, part of the Office of the Dead, and an uncommonly long series of Suffrages. The volume was obviously lacking the beginning of the Office of the Dead and large parts of an unusual and elaborate cycle of Hours and Masses arranged according to the days of the week, but there was no way of knowing what other texts, if any, were missing. Furthermore, since all of the manuscripts with miniatures attributed to the Master of Catherine of Cleves seemed to be intact, there was little reason to expect that the missing portions of the Morgan volume would ever be found.

At this point, the owner of the Guennol volume generously lent his book to us for comparison. It was immediately evident that not only were the two volumes illustrated by the same artist, but also that they were both products of the same scriptorium—the sizes of the leaves, the number of text lines per page, the script, the decoration of the text pages, all were the same. It was not then possible to prove that they were two volumes of the same book, though this appeared to be a strong probability after it was discovered that the Guennol volume was also incomplete. Over the next weeks and months the evidence accumulated. First, it was found that the texts of the volumes complement each other in general to form a Book of Hours of rare, if not unique, complexity and rationality. Next, specific and irrefutable connections were discovered. Frequently the text from a page in one volume runs on directly, sometimes in the middle of a sentence, to a following page in the other volume. Occasionally the titles or rubrics for a text occur in one volume, but the text itself is found in the other (for example, the rubric for the Mass of the Holy Ghost is on page 71 in the Morgan volume, and the text begins on folio 109 of the Guennol

volume). In at least two instances, Morgan p. 178 and Guennol
f.192v, the devious mind that dismembered the book has obliter-
ated the rubrics to disguise the shift in the text from one volume
to the other, although the erasure in the Guennol volume can still
be read under a microscope. The same deviousness led the culprit
to make almost all of the breaks in the middle of gatherings, so
the catchwords at the end of one gathering would run on directly
to the next gathering in the same volume. A different kind of evidence, crucial for restoring to their original positions some of the
full-page miniatures without text on their obverse, consisted of
matching spots or stains found on two once facing pages. From
this evidence it is certain, for instance, that the Meeting at the
Golden Gate (Morgan–p.144) at one time faced the Birth of the
Virgin (Guennol–f.20). The final proof came when the Morgan
volume was removed from its binding; the havoc of severed leaves,
rearranged and pasted together, could be sorted out, and the original, highly regular, gatherings could be reconstructed. The text
and gatherings of the manuscript, as it was presented to Catherine
of Cleves, are reconstructed in Appendix B; the original arrange-
ment of the pictures has been followed in the Descriptions of the
Miniatures, which also contain notes on a few miniatures pre-
sumed to be still missing.

This differs from most reconstructions which rearrange existing
materials and provide further examples of what is already known,
for it incorporates the poorly known Guennol and the almost
completely unknown Morgan volumes into a work of art that is
truly extraordinary in its sustained originality and its consistently
high quality. Indeed, the most important result is this recovery of
a major illuminated manuscript. Beyond this, there are numerous
historical consequences, for the "new" book alters our judgement
of the artist, enlarges our knowledge of Catherine's milieu and of
the potential of contemporary Dutch patronage, and revises our
understanding of the development of Dutch art in the fifteenth
century. The extent of these consequences will not be learned for
years, but in the meantime the following observations, suggestions,
and tentative conclusions will provide further information and
may serve as a point of departure for discussions to come.

Although the addition of the Morgan volume swells the book by almost one hundred miniatures, often with borders of unexampled invention, and greatly extends thereby the recognized range and growth of the artist, it also makes clear the consistency of his decisions and of his taste. Underlying the whole program of illustration, a program which must have taken a number of years to execute, is a remarkable orderliness and rationality. The program must have been worked out from the beginning to avoid redundancy or conflict. The Adoration of the Magi was omitted from the Infancy cycle illustrating the Hours of the Virgin and was reserved for the Suffrage of the Three Kings. Since the Passion cycle had been used for the Hours of the Cross, it was necessary to utilize a different series taken from the Legend of the Cross, and even to invent new scenes, to illustrate the Friday Hours of the Compassion of God and the Mass of the Cross. The same is true of the highly original illustrations for the Saturday Hours and Mass of the Virgin, most of the narrative scenes from the life of the Virgin having been employed to illustrate Her Hours at the beginning of the manuscript. The same logicality is evident within the various cycles, as may be seen in the interplay of the here and hereafter in the Hours of the Dead or of the Mass and its interpretation in the Hours of the Holy Sacrament. The whole program may have been devised with the help of some scholar or cleric, but its execution reveals a mind that delights in systems and in organizing large numbers of things.

This rationality has its formal side. It is apparent in the control of details which never obtrude. One's first impression of the picture of St. Christopher, for example, is limited to the giant figure of the saint and the general landscape of rocks and water; a moment later one becomes aware of the first level of details, such as drapery, rocks, clouds, and sunset sky; but for some time one does not see, not until one uses a magnifying glass, such details as the fish jumping from the water, or the ducks, which measure about one thirty-second of an inch, floating among the reeds. Another aspect of rationality is to be found in the taste for constructed objects, particularly buildings, but also altars, furniture, and the like. We find an interest in how stones are cut and joined together, in how vaults are made and sustained, and in how pieces of stained glass are leaded and supported on armatures. A similar sense of structure underlies the additive compositions of distinct shapes combined in clear patterns. In the Adoration of the Child, for example, the large triangle formed by the parents and the arc of heaven is repeated with variations in the silhouettes of the parents, the roof of the stable, the brick wall, and elsewhere, and at the same time the directions of these lines determine the disposition of many things, as one edge of the roof is paralleled by the weathervane, a bracket, the candle of Joseph, various edges in his and the Virgin's drapery, and even in the drawing of one shepherd's legs. Similarly, the arc of the clouds above is repeated in the wings of the angel, the dormer window in the stable, the shapes of the hills behind, and the way in which the figures of the parents arch towards each other.

The same organizing impulse is revealed in the extended narrative sequences and in the anecdotal details. The desire to tell a story with maximum lucidity leads the artist to portray two successive moments in the scene of Adam sending Seth to Paradise for a branch of the Tree of Mercy (no. 79); Seth is shown twice, once receiving Adam's instructions and again, departing. Similarly, in the Deathbed Scene (no. 41), the heartless and mercenary youth, presumably the son and heir of the dying man, stands aloof from the deathbed, and in the border, where he appears again, he takes money out of the man's money chest. Out of this scene the artist develops three additional stories: the suffering of the soul of the deceased in the mouth of Hell and its final release, the care for the earthly remains of the deceased and the services for his departed spirit, and the subsequent sorrows of the widow, including her pilgrimage, which occur in later borders (nos. 102, 107, 109). The search for elucidation appears in various other ways: in the banderoles and inscriptions to explain an action or to interpret a scene, in the minute pictures and letters in floor-tiles to elaborate the iconography of a portrait, and in the border motifs to reinforce or oppose the meaning of a miniature.

Parallel to the craftsmanship of his own painting is the artist's appreciation of workmanship in various crafts. It is evident in the tools, utensils, stuffs, and other man-made objects that fill many of his paintings, but it is most purely presented in the later "still-life" borders of the manuscript. Products from diverse trades and crafts are included in these borders: wood sculptures, stone carvings, baked goods, fish nets, coins, bird traps and cages, bows and arrows, textiles, and jewelry. All of these objects are executed with a great care for the things themselves and the craftsmanship that produced them, but of them all the artist clearly prefers the more luxurious, particularly the jewelry. The finesse of execution and the enrichment of surfaces shown in the rosary, pins, and necklaces are strikingly like the miniatures, as the luster of the silver, gold, and precious stones is like the luminous translucency of the artist's forms, which seem to glow from within. In fact, he often employs silver and gold in the miniatures, where they never seem foreign substances. He has, indeed, the taste and the instinct for workmanship of a jeweler.

This delight in luxury seems to contrast with, if not to contradict, a more plebeian concern with the homely scenes and everyday objects to be found in the second half of the manuscript, especially in the two miniatures of the Holy Family (nos. 92 and 93), in the marginal scenes of wine drinking and baking (nos. 110 and 111), and in the borders of mussels, fish, and butterflies (nos. 119, 128, and 129). Although the domestic interiors of the Holy Family miniatures are certainly homely, they appear to be the moderately prosperous rooms of a tradesman class. These miniatures are quite different from the marginal genre scenes of peasants or laborers, in which the figures are slightly grotesque with dumpy proportions and sometimes with porcine faces; they and the portrayals of beggars are rather like the unfeeling caricatures of Pieter Bruegel. Such things as mussels, fish, and butterflies may have been everyday objects, but they are coupled with and counterbalanced by exotic objects like the intarsia panels of no. 96. Furthermore such everyday things are transformed into objects of luxury by the way in which they are painted, a fact that is evident in the gold flesh of the mussels or in the stress on iridescence, a quality which all three have in common. Indeed, it is this transmutation of the ordinary into the precious which is characteristic of the artist, and links him with that later Dutch "alchemist," Jan Vermeer.

These traits of the artist may be typical of the manuscript as a whole, but they are more purely embodied in the later than in the earlier miniatures. He shows a very marked development in his style and artistic ideas, moving rapidly toward a greater individuality and originality. One measure of this originality is the creation of the *trompe l'oeil* and still-life borders, which are so novel and so precocious; however, important as these historic innovations are, of still greater importance is the insight gained from watching the creation take place before our eyes, with its alternation of plunging confidence and hesitant withdrawal to tradition.

The development in style can be seen in many details. In an early landscape, such as that in the Meeting at the Golden Gate (no. 4), the ground plane is broken up into a series of sharply tilted and overlapping hills that climb toward a horizon high above the heads of the foreground figures. The scale of objects, such as trees, does not diminish regularly toward the horizon, and the most distant things are far too large and too clearly seen. The landscape formula of successive layers of hills ending at the horizon in one or more domical hills is a convention that goes back at least to the Boucicault Master and to the first years of the fifteenth century. The artist rejected this convention soon, by the time he had completed the Hours of the Virgin, and replaced it with a landscape having a much deeper space, a continuous terrain, a more convincing gradation of scales, a gradient of clarity from the foreground to the background, and a much greater variety of landscape elements distributed through this greater depth. Nevertheless this development cannot be interpreted as a simple growth of realism or an increasing interest in the distance, for after the Hours of the Cross there are relatively few deep landscapes, and the usual outdoor scene has a very shallow foreground landscape with an extremely low horizon line. Despite some striking exceptions, one can distinguish several stages in the artist's changing attitudes toward landscape: a first in which his interest in the distance is limited by a landscape formula; a second in which his

[ 19 ]

interest is matched by a much greater skill in depicting depth; and a third in which the skill is still greater, but the interest is for the most part lacking. It is, of course, in this last stage that he developed the minutely detailed domestic interiors and the life-size still-life borders.

Corresponding to these changes in the landscapes are changes in the representation of the human figure. Perhaps the most obvious change is in the *dramatis personae;* there is a decided increase of human types through a growing discrimination of ages and social classes. In the earlier figures the limbs are differentiated by rather abrupt changes of direction, giving the body a somewhat wooden look, but in the later ones the artist is much more concerned with the ways in which the functional parts are joined together, a concern that gives the body a greater continuity and articulation. The figures are analogous to the paths in the backgrounds of their miniatures: the early paths are broken off at the edge of one hill only to begin again on a hill behind, whereas the later paths wind through the landscapes without breaks. The same correspondence appears in the draperies, whose patterns evolve from angular and broken lines to more flowing and continuous ones. Despite this general movement toward a more integrated and precisely rendered human figure, there is also a counter-movement toward a greater idealization, which is quite evident from the Friday Hours of the Compassion of God onward. The bearing of the figures becomes more graceful and courtly. The modeling of the flesh is softened and diffused; the forms are rounder and fuller; the hair and complexion are usually golden or very blond. The figures increasingly resemble the precious objects of the later borders.

Nothing is known of the Master of Catherine of Cleves other than what can be adduced from this Book of Hours and from other works that can be assigned to him. The greater availability of the Guennol volume has already given rise to new, but as yet unpublished studies of the *oeuvre* of the artist, and now the addition of the Morgan volume and the reconstruction of the original *Horae* have greatly increased the number and variety of works that must be his by definition, have prolonged the period of time during which we know his style with certainty, and have fixed beyond doubt the main directions and stages in the development of his art. Thus the requirements for attributing works to the artist have become more exacting, for any attribution must be able to be interpolated into this development or extrapolated at either end as early or late works. This preliminary report is not the place to discuss at any length these involved and complex questions, but some discussion is inevitable when considering what we know about the artist and the conditions under which this Book of Hours was made.

Several dates have been proposed for the Guennol volume; 1430, about 1435, and circa 1440. The first date was advanced by Friedrich Gorissen a few years ago, and is based on the heraldic shields which occur in the margins of the first two miniatures. These are the eight shields of the great-great-grandfathers of Catherine of Cleves, which are identified in the Descriptions of the Miniatures, nos. 1 and 2, and a ninth and larger shield of Catherine's own. This ninth shield is the critical one. It is divided *per pale* with the Guelders arms of her husband and the Cleves arms of her father, but its crest is that of Cleves rather than Guelders; the latter would be the customary choice after marriage. Mr. Gorissen concludes from the crest that the arms and therefore the manuscript must have have been made between the date of Catherine's marriage on January 26, 1430, and the date on which Catherine actually left Cleves for Guelders, February 4, 1431. Desirable as it would be to have such a precise, fixed date for the book, there are several difficulties in the argument: Gorissen does not support his interpretation of the helm with other examples or heraldic regulations, and the use of the Cleves helm seems to an amateur no more whimsical for a later date than for the year between the marriage and Catherine's move to Guelders; furthermore, it is inconceivable that the original manuscript, as we know it now, could have been made in a single year; and finally, such an early date for the whole book would alter some of our basic notions about the artistic history of this period. It may, however, be possible that the first two miniatures and their armorial borders were executed during the year preceding February 4, 1431 and that the rest of the book was made over quite a few following years with a mean date of about

1435. In all likelihood, such a date cannot be wide of the mark by more than five years.

Some support for this date can be found in a Prayer-book now in The Hague (Meermanno-Westreenianum Museum 10.E.1), which has twelve miniatures accepted by most students as the work of the Cleves Master. Several do resemble in a general way the miniatures in Catherine's *Horae,* and indeed the painting of St. Michael is almost identical in individual forms and in composition to no. 101; yet the loose manner of painting, the indistinctness of form, the neglect of details, and the awkwardness of articulation occur nowhere in the Cleves Hours. One might take the Prayer-book for an early pastiche by the master, even though such an opinion would contradict the meticulous craftsmanship that characterizes the Cleves Hours from beginning to end, except for the fact that some features are too advanced to be found in his early works. An example of this is the atmospheric, almost Chinese, representation of distant hills floating in the sky of the St. Michael picture, a manner of representation not found in the Cleves *Horae* until after the Hours of the Virgin. Given this evidence, the miniatures in the Prayer-book must be products of the master's workshop or the work of a follower. That one of these is the case is further indicated by the technique of transferring a design from a model to the vellum leaf by means of pricking and then drawing between these points, a technique that can be most clearly seen in the Prayer-book's Last Judgement miniature, but was used in most, if not all, of the others. The attribution of these miniatures is crucial for the date of Catherine's manuscript, since the Prayer-book is firmly dated 1438. If the miniatures were by the master, then the Cleves Hours would have to be later, considerably later, at least in the 1440's. But if, as we believe, these miniatures are the work of a follower, then the St. Michael composition, and perhaps others in the Cleves Hours, must have been in existence before 1438. This would tend to confirm a date for the Cleves Hours of about 1435.

Although all of the miniatures with their borders appear to be the work of the master, three different hands worked on the rather simple decoration that occurs on nearly all of the text pages. For the most part, these decorations consist of a vertical gold bar at the left of the text, which extends to the upper and lower margins and from each end of which a leaf grows horizontally across the top and bottom of the page. In two different sections (for example, Guennol ff. 91v–106v and Morgan pp. 102–112) human figures or animals or little scenes are added to the leaves by two distinct hands, one of which is very close to the master himself. It is possible that these hands can be connected with miniatures in other manuscripts, and thus we may eventually be able to identify the Cleves Master's assistants in this project. We already know that he worked with other artists on at least two other manuscripts, the two vernacular Dutch Bibles in the British Museum (Add. 15410 and Add. 38122). A careful study of these associated artists and of the decorators and scribes involved should yield an accurate and fairly detailed picture of the circumstances under which the Cleves Master developed and practiced his art. In all probability he worked in Utrecht, and perhaps some further information may be adduced from the calendar of Catherine's *Horae,* now in the Morgan volume and here transcribed in Appendix C, which is for use in the diocese of Utrecht although it differs in a number of entries from the available Utrecht calendars.

As a consequence of the new knowledge provided by the Morgan volume and the reconstruction of the whole manuscript, it will be necessary to reconsider all of the proposals that have been made about the sources of the Cleves Master's art and its influence. It has been said, for example, that the master was a pupil of the Dutch artist known as the Master of Zweder van Culemborg, in part because the Cleves Master has been thought to have contributed some miniatures at the end of one of the Zweder Master's major works, the Egmond Breviary in the Morgan Library (M.87). If, however, one places the two books side by side, the differences are more striking than the similarities, and furthermore the earliest miniatures in the Cleves Hours are less like the Zweder Master's work than are some of the later ones. Thus, it seems impossible that he was the teacher of the Cleves Master.

The sources of some of the master's compositions, as has been pointed out by several writers, are to be found in Flemish panel painting. The example most often mentioned is the Descent from the Cross (no. 28) which follows in general a composition of the Master of Flémalle preserved in a copy belonging to the Walker Art Gallery in Liverpool, though it deviates in many details. Nevertheless, the total number of such "quotations" is relatively small; many compositions are drawn from other sources, mostly manuscript sources; and the number of seemingly original compositions is very large. Among the other sources from outside the Netherlands are the works of the Boucicaut Master and particularly the Master of the *Grandes Heures de Rohan*. To the latter has been attributed a drawing in the Herzog Anton Ulrich Museum, Braunschweig, which has identical figures and the same general composition as the Pool of Bethesda (no. 86). Occasionally single figures, such as the Saul in no. 131 or the seated beggar in no. 135, look like the very distinctive types of the Rohan Master. These are only a few of the sources of the Cleves Hours that students will find, but whatever we may learn eventually in this area, it seems certain that our artist was very cosmopolitan, that he drew on a wide range of sources, as every intelligent artist of every age does, and that he transformed these borrowings to conform to his own taste and ideas, as any great artist must.

# DESCRIPTIONS OF THE MINIATURES

In the following descriptions, the 157 miniatures are numbered in sequence according to their order in the reconstructed manuscript. Below each number is a letter in brackets: L indicates a full-page miniature measuring about 6½ x 4¼ inches with its border, and S means a smaller miniature set in the text and measuring 2¼ x 2½ inches without the border. Following each number is a brief iconographic title, and then, in parentheses, comes the volume designation, G for Guennol or M for Morgan, and the Guennol folio number or the Morgan page number. Inasmuch as every section of the text is introduced by one or more miniatures, the name of each section has been inserted before the first of its miniatures. Where the terms "right" and "left" are used, these are the spectator's right and left, unless otherwise specified.

## *Hours of the Virgin—Matins*

1. CATHERINE OF CLEVES KNEELING BEFORE THE VIRGIN AND CHILD.
[L] (G – f.1v) The crowned Virgin stands on an inverted silver crescent moon. She holds her Child and an ink bottle into which He dips His pen. Across His lap lies an illegible scroll, and an empty scroll case hangs over the arm of the Virgin. Both figures, encompassed by a gold mandorla, are placed within a shallow chapel, possibly Catherine's own, surmounted by flying buttresses, crenelations, two turrets with music-making angels, and, in the central niche, a statue that blesses and holds a gold object (a church ?) in its arm. Beneath the statue hangs a heraldic shield *à bouche,* Barry of eight argent and sable. Catherine kneels at the Virgin's right with an open book and a banderole inscribed *O mater dei memento mei.* Along with Catherine's arms, the border has those of four of her great-great-grandfathers—Count Diderik of Cleves, Count Engelbert of Mark, Duke Ludwig of Bavaria, and Duke Ludwig of Liegnitz. The arms of her other great-great-grandfathers appear on the facing page. [PLATE 3]

2. ANNUNCIATION TO JOACHIM. (G – f.2) Joachim, his hands in
[s] prayer, kneels before a small flying angel with a blank scroll. In
the field behind him and in the warren on the right are many
rabbits, symbolic of a fecundity heretofore denied the old man.
The border contains, among other things, a "wild man" stalking
a hare, a stag, and the arms of Catherine's four remaining great-
great-grandfathers—those of Jean le Bon, King of France, Count
Lodewijk of Flanders, Duke Wilhelm of Jülich, and Duke Otto of
Ravensberg. [PLATE 4]

## Hours of the Virgin—Lauds

3. THREE SINGING ANGELS. (G– f.11) While singing, the angels
[s] kneel or sit on the floor and hold open a scroll with the beginning
words of the hymn: *Te deum laudamus.* The unusual border is
composed of golden peas in open pods. (As symbols of fertility,
they probably referred originally to a facing full-page miniature,
now missing, of the Annunciation to St. Anne.)

## Hours of the Virgin—Prime

4. MEETING AT THE GOLDEN GATE. .(M – p.144) In style this mini-
[L] ature clearly belongs among the earliest paintings of the manuscript, and in theme it ought to follow the Annunciation to St.
Anne and to precede the Birth of the Virgin. That it originally
faced the page with the Birth of the Virgin is proved by a number
of small brown stains along the inner margins of both pages which
match perfectly. Joachim and Anne embrace with restraint outside the walls of the gate of Jerusalem depicted as a small gold
door, partly open, in the reddish walls of the city. Above the gate
are two turrets topped by fanciful vase-like forms. [PLATE 5]

5. BIRTH OF THE VIRGIN. (G – f.20) St. Anne is seated in a bed
[s] with red covers and red canopy, except for the center which is blue
with gold stars. (The same canopy appears in the Death of the
Virgin, no. 14.) She receives the swaddled Virgin from the midwife.
Opposite a cat washes and warms itself before a fire; on the far wall
is a convex mirror, and through the wall a window opens to a

distant landscape. The lower border contains two beehives, a reference to the Immaculate Conception, since bees were thought to procreate without intercourse.

## Hours of the Virgin—Terce

6. PRESENTATION OF THE VIRGIN IN THE TEMPLE. (G – f.23v) The
[L] young Virgin climbs unaided the 15 steps to the Temple where are seated the priest Zacharias and, before him, two small virgins weaving and sewing. Beside the stairs, in a "courtyard," stand the Virgin's parents, Joachim holding a string of amber-colored beads.

7. DESIGNATION OF JOSEPH. (G – f.24) The seven suitors for the
[S] hand of the Virgin stand before the high priest and the altar, but the selection of Joseph has already occurred—the dove of the Holy Ghost hovers over his head, and another suitor, holding Joseph's branched staff, points to him. Having turned away from the altar, the slumping Joseph is supported by a fellow suitor. Another suitor has turned his back on the scene—apparently in disappointment.

## Hours of the Virgin—Sext

8. MARRIAGE OF THE VIRGIN. (G–f.27v) Facing front, Joseph stands
[L] in the center of the scene and is flanked by the high priest, on the left, and by the Virgin, on the right. The priest blesses the marriage by placing his hand over the joined hands of the bride and groom. Among the attendants is a man with a greenish face who peers dourly over the shoulder of Joseph at the joined hands. The scene takes place within a brick- and rib-vaulted temple, which appears to be domed on the outside with two fanciful flying buttresses reaching up to a rectangular "cupola."

9. DISPATCHING THE ANGEL OF THE ANNUNCIATION. (G–f.28) Two
[S] angels stand before God, who wears a high conical hat and holds a golden orb on His knee. From His right hand unrolls a banderole with Isaiah's prophecy of the coming of the Saviour as quoted by Christ at His entry into Jerusalem: *Dicite filiae syon Ecce rex tuus venit* . . . (Tell ye the daughter of Sion, Behold, thy King cometh . . .).

The eyes of God look toward the angel on His right, who appears in the Annunciation that follows.

## Hours of the Virgin—None

10. ANNUNCIATION TO THE VIRGIN. (G–f.31v) Seated demurely with
[L] an open book in Her lap, the Virgin faces Gabriel, who kneels
before Her holding a staff and a scroll with the angelic salutation.
At Her side is a lectern and bookcase with a metal basin, symbolic
of the Virgin's purity, as is the vase of lilies in the foreground. The
scene takes place in a tall vaulted building, possibly the temple,
since the roof is topped by two golden crescents of the type often,
but not exclusively, used in representations of the temple. Hanging from the frame, however, are two St. George shields, argent,
a cross-couped gules.                                    [PLATE 6]

11. VISITATION. (G – f.32)   The meeting of the Virgin and Elizabeth
[S] occurs just outside the latter's house, a red stone building. Instead
of embracing or examining the signs of each other's pregnancy,
they clasp hands restrainedly as they do in some other Utrecht
manuscripts. In the lower border are the two naked infants; John
the Baptist is trapping birds with nets, decoys, and caged birds,
while Christ sits between the two nets. This scene refers to the
Incarnation and the trap of the flesh.

## Hours of the Virgin—Vespers

12. ADORATION OF THE CHILD.   (G – f.35v)   Outside the stable kneel
[L] the parents of the Infant, who lies naked on a white cloth between
them. Joseph holds a burning candle. The stone and timber stable
is well thatched and in quite good repair. In the middle distance
an angel in the luminous yellow sky announces the Nativity to
two shepherds, and in the reddish haze of the far distance can be
seen the buildings of Bethlehem.                        [PLATE 7]

13. FLIGHT INTO EGYPT. (G – f.36)   The Holy Family, with Joseph
[S] leading the ass on which the Virgin rides and holds the swaddled
Child, is entering a rocky defile. None of the miracles associated

with the Flight are shown. In the lower border is a woman churning.

## Hours of the Virgin—Compline

14. DEATH OF THE VIRGIN. (M – p.156) The twelve Apostles are
[L] crowded around the red-draped bed of the dying Virgin. She holds
a burning candle with St. Peter, who has an aspergillum in his other
hand. St. Paul reads from an open book, and another apostle holds
a censer. On the blue ceiling of the canopy are gold stars.

15. ASSUMPTION OF THE VIRGIN. (G – f.42) The central and frontal
[S] Virgin hovers between heaven and earth, while standing on a silver
crescent moon and within a yellow mandorla. She is crowned, and
her hands are in an attitude of prayer. In the small arc of heaven
above are God, blessing and holding a globe, and orange cherubim.

## Hours of the Cross—Matins

16. AGONY IN THE GARDEN. (M – p.120) Before a hillock forming a
[L] natural altar with chalice and wafer, Christ kneels in prayer and
looks up to the arc of heaven from which the Father leans out blessing and offering a cross to His Son. Three apostles sit or recline in
the foreground, but only Peter seems to sleep. This scene is enclosed by a woven fence in which there is an open, though covered,
gate. Neither Jerusalem nor approaching soldiers are to be seen
in the deep and detailed landscape behind. Among the border
figures is a symbolic pelican feeding her young with the blood from
her breast.

17. TAKING OF CHRIST. (G – f.47) With his hands on the head and
[S] neck of Christ, Judas does not fully embrace Him, nor does he kiss
Him. Christ reaches down blindly to restore the ear of the bleeding
soldier above whom Peter still stands with raised sword. The row
of soldiers behind blocks out any landscape, except the yellow sky.

## Hours of the Cross—Lauds

18. CHRIST BEFORE CAIAPHAS. (G – f.52v) Christ, His long sleeves
[L] covering His hands and bound wrists, stands before the enthroned

[ 29 ]

Caiaphas who wears a hooded mantle. Before both kneels a "jester."
Behind Christ are soldiers, one of whom holds Him around the
middle, and Peter who is denying Him. The room has a yellowish
(wooden ?) barrel-vault. In the lower margin, a repentant Peter
weeps at the mouth of a cave.                                    [PLATE 8]

19. MOCKING OF CHRIST.   (G – f.53)   Seated in the center, His head
[s]  covered by a white cloth, Christ is mocked by four men, while
Caiaphas stands by. One of the four blows a trumpet at Him, while
the others gesture and grimace. The scene is laid in a gray groin-
vaulted room. In the margin, but as an extension of the scene,
a figure beats a metal basin with a stick.

## Hours of the Cross—Prime

20. CHRIST BEFORE PILATE.   (M – p.38)   Pilate, wearing a ballooned-
[L]  crown hat, sits on a throne in his barrel-vaulted audience hall. An
attendant pours water into a basin, while Pilate washes his hands.
Facing him are Christ, dressed and standing as He did before
Caiaphas, and a group of soldiers. On the rear wall is a Dutch
inscription: *Versinnet dat Ende*. In the border behind Pilate, a
figure empties a jar of water (?) into a dragon's mouth.

21. CHRIST BEFORE HEROD.   (G – f.58)   As Christ stood in front of
[s]  Caiaphas, He now stands before Herod, who sits upon his throne
with crown and sceptre. There are only two attendants; the soldiers
have disappeared.

## Hours of the Cross—Terce

22. FLAGELLATION OF CHRIST.   (G – f.60v)   While Pilate watches,
[L]  Christ is tied to the mauve-rose column by two men. Of the two
remaining men, one holds Christ by the head and draws back his
fist to hit Him, while the other raises with both hands a bundle of
branches with which to strike Him. The almost completely naked
body of Christ is covered with bleeding scratches.       [PLATE 9]

23. BUFFETING OF CHRIST.   (G – f.61)   Dressed again in His long-
[s]  sleeved robe and with His hands tied, but blindfolded and crowned

with thorns, Christ sits in the middle of five men who torment Him. Two of these men strike Him with long staves, while Pilate watches in the background.

## Hours of the Cross—Sext

24. CHRIST CARRYING THE CROSS. (G – f.63v) In addition to the
[L] cross, Christ is encumbered by two large metal clogs or spikeblocks hung apparently from His waist, but He is assisted by one man who supports the arm of the cross on his shoulders. They are followed by St. John and the Virgin and are accompanied by three soldiers, one of whom leads Him by a rope fastened around His waist. In the margin St. Veronica displays the cloth with the image of the Holy Face. [PLATE 10]

25. PREPARATION OF THE CROSS. (G – f.64) Christ, His body naked
[s] and bleeding, sits with His wrists bound, while two men nail and drill into the cross. On the left, the Virgin and St. John (?) watch the preparations.

## Hours of the Cross—None

26. CRUCIFIXION. (G – f.66v) The smooth, frontal cross of the dead
[L] Christ stands between and slightly in front of the two rough, foreshortened crosses of the thieves. The arms of the thieves are brought over the tops of the horizontal arms of their crosses and tied behind. The body of the thief on Christ's right has a pinkish color, and although his face looks up, his eyes are covered by a cloth band; the body of the other thief is yellowish, his wrists are bound to a short stick, and he turns his ugly face and uncovered eyes away from Christ. Below, St. John supports the swooning Virgin, while Mary Magdalene stands passively by. Opposite, three of the four spectators and soldiers look up at Christ; from the pointing hand of the centurion unrolls a scroll inscribed: *Vere filius dei est iste* (Truly this is the Son of God). Above Christ, in an arc of heaven, is His Father surrounded by angels. In the lower border, directly beneath Christ, is a kneeling angel, weeping. [PLATE 11]

27. JOSEPH OF ARIMATHAEA BEFORE PILATE. (G – f.67) Joseph,
[s] the "rich man of Arimathaea," bends forward with his hat removed as he approaches the enthroned Pilate from whom he begs
for the body of Jesus. Behind Joseph is Nicodemus, who is about
to remove his hat. Two attendants on Pilate's right complete the
group set in a small flat-roofed room. In the lower margin a hunter
on foot sounds his horn, as he follows his hounds chasing a rabbit.

## Hours of the Cross—Vespers

28. DESCENT FROM THE CROSS. (G – f.69v) Standing at the top of
[L] the ladder, the bare-headed Nicodemus holds the body of Christ
under the arms and lowers it into the arms of an assistant. The
Magdalene, her back turned, watches the lowering from below.
St. John supports the swooning Virgin at the left, as in the Cruci-
fixion. Behind this group and somewhat removed is Joseph of
Arimathaea, who holds a jar of ointment and watches the descent.
Two angels hover in the distance.                          [PLATE 12]

29. LAMENTATION AND ANOINTING. (G – f.70) Seated below the
[s] cross, the Virgin holds the upper part of Christ's body in her lap,
while the kneeling Joseph, his hands covered by a white cloth,
holds and anoints Christ's feet, and Nicodemus anoints His left
arm in the same way. Several jars of ointment lie on the ground.
Behind the Virgin are a prayerful St. John and a frantic Magdalene
wringing her hands, which she raises over her head.

## Hours of the Cross—Compline

30. ENTOMBMENT. (G – f.73v) The body of Christ, lying in a white
[L] winding sheet, is held over the open sarcophagus by Nicodemus
(at the head?) and Joseph (at the foot?). From behind the mauve-
rose sarcophagus, the Virgin leans forward and raises Christ's left
hand to her face. The Magdalene, with a jar of ointment, and the
two Holy Women stand in back of the Virgin. In the foreground
lies the stone of unction or lid of the sarcophagus with two ointment jars.                                                 [PLATE 13]

31. RESURRECTION. (G–f.74)  The lid has been twisted across the
[s] open sarcophagus, out of which steps Christ holding His cross-staff
and banner. Around the tomb are three soldiers sleeping in awk-
ward positions and the centurion with half-open eyes.

## Sunday Hours of the Trinity—Matins

32. TRINITY IN AN APSE. (G–f.77v)  The three persons of the Trinity
[L] are seated on a red throne in a rib-vaulted apse supported by flying
buttresses on the outside and decorated with finials, gold banners,
and a gold crescent. The Son, seated in the middle and facing
directly forward, blesses and holds a book on His knee; the Father,
an old man crowned with a tiara and holding a gold globe on
His knee, extends one arm behind His Son's back; and the Holy
Ghost, upon whose halo is perched a dove, is somewhat more youthful than Christ, whom He partially embraces and whose book He
helps to hold. In the left and lower borders is an L-shaped band
of orange-colored angels surrounded by yellow clouds, which appear to have been repainted, but have merely lost most of the
blue pigment applied originally over much of the yellow.

[PLATE 14]

33. GOD THE FATHER. (G–f.78)  Seated frontally on a large red
[s] throne, the Father is dressed as before (no. 32) and wears the same
conical tiara. One hand is raised in blessing; the other holds a
globe on His knee. Two yellow angels appear behind in brown
clouds which open to show gold stars in a blue sky. In the border,
a goat stretches up to eat a cluster of grapes.

## Sunday Hours of the Trinity—Prime

34. GOD THE SON. (G–f.80v)  The figure of Christ is identical with
[s] the one in the previous miniature of the Trinity (no. 32), but He is
here seated alone on a large red throne. In the border is a music-
making angel.

## Sunday Hours of the Trinity—Terce

35. TRINITY ENTHRONED. (G–f.82)  Sitting on a red throne in the
[s] sky, the three persons of the Trinity are depicted as before (no. 32),

except for the Holy Ghost, who now has His own book and lacks His dove. The sky behind is blue with gold stars, and around the edge of the largely elliptical frame are angels in various colors. All three Persons have scrolls with difficult-to-read inscriptions on death and salvation.

## Sunday Hours of the Trinity—Sext

36. TRINITY WITH THE SON KNEELING. (G – f.83v) The Son no
[s] longer sits on the large red throne with His Father and the Holy Ghost, but kneels instead on the step in front of His vacant seat. Christ is blessed by His Father and accepts a golden cross from Him. In the lower border a woman holds a rooster which she prepares to pluck, and a monkey ladles some kind of liquid from a bowl.

## Sunday Hours of the Trinity—None

37. TRINITY WITH DOVE AND INFANT CHRIST. (G – f.85) From the
[s] tiara-crowned Father, who blesses and holds a globe in an arc of heaven above, radiate golden rays along which descend, toward the landscape below, the dove of the Holy Ghost and the naked infant Christ holding a cross. This type of Trinity belongs normally to the Annunciation to the Virgin. A further reference to the Incarnation occurs in the lower border where a fisherman kneels on the bank of a small pond in and around which are various kinds of nets, traps, and other equipment for fishing.

## Sunday Hours of the Trinity—Vespers

38. THRONE-OF-GRACE TRINITY. (G–f.86v) Seated on a gray throne,
[s] the bareheaded Father holds the cross with His crucified Son, from whose feet blood flows onto a golden globe of the earth below. The dove of the Holy Ghost hovers between the heads of the other two Persons. In the lower border are the two spies of Moses returning from Canaan with the gigantic cluster of grapes carried on a staff between them (a common antetype for the Crucifixion); their two scrolls give part of their report on the land of milk and honey (Numbers XIII, 27).

## Sunday Hours of the Trinity—Compline

39. TRINITY WITH SON SHOWING WOUNDS. (G – f.88) As the two
[s] preceding miniatures show the Trinity at the Incarnation and
Crucifixion, this shows them after the Crucifixion. The Son in the
center is supported by the other two Persons, who appear as before
(e.g. no. 32); the wounds on His half-naked body are displayed;
His feet rest on the gold globe of the earth; and His cross is held
before Him by the Holy Ghost.

## Mass of the Trinity

40. TRINITY ADORED. (G – f.90) Appearing in an arc of heaven
[s] above is a Trinity of the Throne-of-Grace type, except that the
Father is only bust length. Below are eight kneeling religious and
lay men, including a pope, two cardinals, a bishop, and three men
in armor, of whom one is dressed in gold—his cape has a black
double-headed eagle, and his helmet carries a crown and a cross.
In the borders are an owl and a grazing stag. A now missing full-
page miniature probably faced this page originally.

## Monday Hours of the Dead—Matins

41. DEATHBED SCENE. (M – p.180) In a narrow room the bed of
[L] a dying man divides the background figures from the two seated in
the foreground, a cowled priest (?) who reads at a table with numerous vessels and other objects, presumably for the Viaticum or
Extreme Unction, and a black-garbed woman, probably the widow,
who prays over an open book. Behind the bed are two women, one
who tends the dying man and the other who helps him to hold
a burning candle, a physician examining a urine specimen, and,
somewhat apart, a foppish companion and the mercenary heir, who
appears again in the lower border taking money bags out of a
coffer. Dominating the rear wall of the room is a large window,
shuttered except for one section, through which is seen a very distant landscape. That this miniature introduces the Hours of the
Dead is proved by the transfer of two brown stains from folio 97
in the Guennol volume. [PLATE 15]

42. HELLMOUTH WITH TORMENTED SOULS. (G – f.97) Filling the
[s] miniature is a monstrous head of Hell, almost black with yellow
and orange flames or lights, heightened with gold radiating from
its eyes and ears. Its fanged and flaming crimson mouth holds seven
souls, naked and youthful, contorted in anguish and praying.

## Monday Hours of the Dead—Prime

43. PREPARATION OF THE CORPSE OF THE DECEASED. (G – f.99v)
[s] The naked corpse of the man dying in the earlier deathbed scene
is being lowered in a white winding sheet onto some straw on the
floor by two men. The bare room appears to be that of the deathbed scene with a few alterations, resulting in part from the different shape and size of this miniature. The shutters on the
window have been thrown open revealing a larger landscape in
the distance.

## Monday Hours of the Dead—Terce

44. OFFICE OF THE DEAD. (G–f.101) The coffin on the left, covered
[s] with a red cloth and supporting two candles, has been placed
before the altar on the right, which has one candle visible. Behind
the coffin are two kneeling mourners clothed in black, and just
behind them in a choir stall are three singing clerics; each is wearing a surplice and one has a horned hood.

## Monday Hours of the Dead—Sext

45. INTERMENT OF THE DECEASED. (G – f.102v) While two men
[s] lower the wooden coffin into the grave, the priest in white surplice
sprinkles holy water from an aspergillum onto the coffin. Four
mourners in black stand behind the grave.

## Monday Hours of the Dead—None

46. REQUIEM MASS FOR THE DECEASED. (G – f.104) With his back
[s] to us and facing the altar, the priest prays. The altar has curtains,
gold retable, and other fixtures. Besides the priest, there are three

mourners in black, one of whom kneels at the side of the altar and offers a silver or pewter vessel to an attendant, who has already placed two gifts (bread ?) on the altar.

## Monday Hours of the Dead–Vespers

47. HELLMOUTH WITH THREE SOULS AT A TABLE. (G–f.105v) Within
[s] the hellmouth, conceived and painted as before, is a long bare table, at which three naked souls kneel, with their hands in prayer. An angel flies down to the table with a cloth containing small brown objects that look like the bread (?) placed on the altar in the preceding miniature.

## Monday Hours of the Dead–Compline

48. RELEASE OF SOULS FROM THE HELLMOUTH. (G – f.107) A
[s] walking angel leads five naked souls out of the mouth of hell, which is identical with the one described above. In the lower border a hunter is catching birds with a string trap; below the trap are two caged birds serving as decoys, and in the distance is an open cage waiting for the quarry.

## Mass of the Dead

49. LAST JUDGEMENT. (M – p.28) The triangular composition is
[L] dominated by three main figures: at the apex is Christ seated on a rainbow-like arc; on the ground below are the Virgin and John the Baptist kneeling in adoration. In front of the latter two are naked figures emerging from the earth. From the distant waters, seen between the Virgin and St. John, rises a rocky island, on top of which rest the golden globe of the earth surmounted by a cross; in a fissure of the island is a red demon. Two groups of bust-length saints are placed at the ends of heaven's arc, flanking Christ.

Out of the upper corners descend two orange angels, each blowing a long trumpet from which flutters a St. George banner (argent, a cross-couped gules). Lilies and a sword extend from the mouth of Christ. In the four corners of the elaborate border are medal-

lions with the Evangelist Symbols identified by scrolls with their
names. [FRONTISPIECE. PLATE 1]

50. St. michael weighing souls. (M – p.29) St. Michael, dressed
[s] in golden armor, holds a long red staff topped by a gold cross in
his left hand, and the gold scales in his right. The left cup of the
scales holds a naked prayerful soul, while a roseate demon tampers
with the other cup. A music-making angel and a crane-like bird
appear in the border.

## Tuesday Hours of the Holy Ghost—Matins

51. Pentecost. (M – p.52) The descent of the Holy Ghost onto
[L] the Virgin and twelve Apostles takes place in the apse of a church
which is vaulted in a strange manner. The ceiling is mainly a barrel
vault with transverse ribs, but also with liernes; it rests on a horizontal moulding which, in turn, is carried on the apexes of pointed
wall arches. Along the moulding are small armorial shields. In
contrast to the generally white interior, some of the vaulting ribs
are red and are arranged so that they echo the descent of the Holy
Ghost whose white dove is perched on the Virgin's head. Around
the dove is diffused a reddish radiance against Her white, not gold,
halo. Also emanating from the dove toward the Apostles are gold
rays, a pattern that is repeated in the halos of gold radiating lines
about the Apostles' heads. In addition to the halos, they have the
customary red flames on top of their heads. Although surrounded
by the Apostles, the Virgin remains calmly aloof from their agita-
tion and absorbed in Her reading. Around the interior scene is a
framework of roofs, finials, flags, and buttresses. [PLATE 16]

52. Wisdom: judgement of solomon. (M – p.53) Illustrating
[s] wisdom, the first of the gifts of the Holy Ghost, is Solomon's method
of determination of the true mother of a disputed child by threaten-
ing to cut him in two. With the dove of the Holy Ghost perched
on his head, Solomon sits upon his throne and holds his sword
over the infant's naked body. Kneeling before him is the real
mother, who pleads with the king and offers to surrender her child
to the other woman, who stands behind with two court attendants.

In the lower border is a baby asleep in his cradle; in the upper margin is an inscription explaining that wisdom restored the child to his mother.

## Tuesday Hours of the Holy Ghost—Prime

53. UNDERSTANDING: DAVID (?) KNEELING BEFORE AN ALTAR. (M–p.57)
[s] The second gift, understanding or *intellectus,* is illustrated by a gray-haired, gray-bearded man who kneels in prayer on the step of an altar. Above him is a banderole which asks in Latin, "Give me understanding that I may learn your commandments." This is almost a direct quote from Psalm CXVIII, 34 (Vulgate numeration), and therefore the man is probably David. Flying over the altar is the dove of the Holy Ghost with a Latin scroll saying, "I shall give you understanding." The top of the altar is bare except for an altar cloth. At the back is a retable in three sections, each with a panel of gold and a candle in front. Behind is an open door through which may be seen a landscape vista.

## Tuesday Hours of the Holy Ghost—Terce

54. COUNSEL: KING AND ADVISERS TAKING COUNSEL. (M – p.60)
[s] A king, perhaps Solomon, stands in counsel with three advisers. The dove of the Holy Ghost alights on the king's head, while he expounds. He holds a book in his left hand. In the lower border is a large bird standing on burning logs; the Latin legend in the upper margin reads, "*Consilium: Ibi salus ubi multa consilia.*"

## Tuesday Hours of the Holy Ghost—Sext

55. FORTITUDE: JACOB STRUGGLES WITH AN ANGEL. (M – p.73) The
[s] fourth gift of the Holy Ghost is represented by Jacob's conquest of the angel. While Joseph holds his wrist and garment, the angel struggles to get away, and points toward the sky. The sense of the scene is explained by the quotation in the upper margin of Genesis XXXII, 26, which in the King James version reads: "And he [the angel] said, Let me go, for the day breaketh. And he [Jacob] said, I will not let thee go. . . ." The action takes place in front of a red

[ 39 ]

building; there is no sign of the river Jabbok. The angel, wearing a gold halo, amice, stole, and maniple, appears to represent the church; Jacob has no halo, but over his head flies the dove of the Holy Ghost.

## Tuesday Hours of the Holy Ghost—None

56. KNOWLEDGE: TEACHER AND PUPILS. (M – p.62) This school-
[s] room scene depicts the fifth gift of the Holy Ghost. The seated teacher holds a whip in one hand and in the other an open book, which he extends for the recitation of the student kneeling before him. Over the student's head is the dove of the Holy Ghost and a banderole with a quotation in Latin from Psalm II, 12, saying in part, "Embrace discipline." Two other students studying their books are seated on the straw-strewn floor. The grotto-like room has two barred windows in its inward curving walls.

## Tuesday Hours of the Holy Ghost—Vespers

57. PIETY: LADY DISTRIBUTING ALMS. (M – p.65) Piety, the sixth
[s] of the gifts of the Holy Ghost, is interpreted as charity. Outside the door of her house or palace, a fashionably dressed lady gives money to three beggars. The lady seems to be a conventionalized portrait of Catherine of Cleves, since she is very like, and even wears the same chatelaine as, the portrait with the Crucifix (no. 96). While reaching into her purse with one hand, she puts a coin into one beggar's bowl with the other. The two remaining beggars also hold out bowls; one is crippled and uses a crutch, and all are tattered and patched. The dove of the Holy Ghost hovers over the head of the lady, and the banderole above the beggars' heads gives a quotation from Luke XI, 41 which reads in translation, "Give alms, and all things are clean unto you." In the lower border, a woman kneels beside the barred prison window of Christ and gives Him a dish.

## Tuesday Hours of the Holy Ghost—Compline

58. FEAR OF THE LORD. (M – p.68) Arranged in a triangular com-
[s] position, like that of the Last Judgement (no. 49), are Christ, a

kneeling gentleman, possibly Arnold of Guelders, and a standing demon. Christ has all of his attributes as the judge: lilies, sword, crown of thorns, wounds, rainbow, and golden globe below. The gentleman, his broad-brimmed hat on the ground in front of him, prays to Christ, while the dove of the Holy Ghost hovers over him. With bat wings on shoulders and hips, hellmouth head, and a strange yellow lattice-work on his abdomen, the demon gesticulates like a prosecutor. All three have banderoles with biblical quotations concerning fear of the Lord: the gentleman's from Psalm CXVIII, 120 (Vulgate), the demon's from Psalm XXXV, 2 (Vulgate), and Christ's from Ecclesiastes XII, 13. In the upper margin is a Latin legend which says that fear of the Lord is the beginning of wisdom.

## Mass of the Holy Ghost

59. St. peter bestowing the holy ghost. (M – p.72) The mean-
[L] ing of this rare, if not unique, scene, is given in the legend at the top of the page, a quotation from Acts VIII, 17, here changed to exclude John and to stress Peter (and by implication the Roman Church). The biblical passage tells how Peter and John conveyed the Holy Ghost to the people of Samaria by placing their hands on them. In the center of the scene, Peter places his hand, with the dove of the Holy Ghost perched on it, upon the head of the first of four men kneeling before him. Standing behind Peter are three more men, two of whom are graybeards. The nearest of these seems sceptical and is probably Simon Magus, who appears in the next miniature. The scene occurs in an open octagonal tempietto supported by thin columns and covered with a rib vaulting. Through the open sides can be seen a deep landscape which reaches to the distant sea where a sailing ship rides at anchor. Around the picture is a border of fleshy, squid-shaped plants.          [plate 17]

60. Simon seeks to buy the power of peter. (G – f.109) Im-
[s] pressed with Peter's apparent power to bestow the Holy Ghost on men, Simon the Magician offers Peter money. Simon, dressed as in the preceding miniature except that he now wears a long-brim hat, holds out the money to Peter, who refuses with one hand and

[ 41 ]

holds a book in the other. Between the two hovers the dove of the Holy Ghost. The scene is explained by the legend in the upper border composed of quotations from Acts VIII, 19–20 (the legend substitutes *gratiam* for *potestatem*). In the border, a boy shears a lamb on his lap.

## Wednesday Hours of All Saints—Matins

61. ALL SAINTS BEFORE GOD THE FATHER. (G – f.115v) Suspended
[L] in the air above the standing assemblage of saints is the throne of God the Father. He is seated frontally, wears a blue and gold tiara, blesses with one hand, and holds a book with the other; over His head hangs a conical canopy. The saints are separated into two groups: at the left are Sts. Thomas Apostle, George, John the Baptist, a pope, and a cardinal; at the right are Sts. Jerome, Agnes, Cecilia, and two other female saints. Three banderoles, one for each group of saints and one for God the Father, are adapted from Psalm LX, 4–8, and speak God's legacy to and support for the saints. Forming a border for the scene is a row of nine flaming angels in blue clouds.                                    [PLATE 18]

62. VIRGIN KNEELING BEFORE CHRIST. (M – p.39) This composi-
[S] tion is customarily reserved for scenes of the Virgin's coronation, but here there is no crowning. Christ, with gold crown and orb, is seated at the right of a large double throne, and He blesses the Virgin, who kneels in adoration on the floor in front of Her empty seat. The throne is covered by a textile brightly patterned with gold crowns, each encircling three feathers, and with pairs of facing swans or white geese.

## Wednesday Hours of All Saints—Prime

63. ANGELS ADORE GOD THE FATHER. (G – f.116) Enthroned fron-
[S] tally, wearing a blue and gold tiara, and with His hands blessing and holding a gold globe, the Father is flanked by two groups of three standing angels. Each group has a banderole, which combine to give the first two verses of the ancient hymn, *Te Deum*.

## Wednesday Hours of All Saints—Terce

64. APOSTLES AND PROPHETS ADORING GOD THE FATHER. (G–f.117v)

[s] The Father is identical with the portrayal in the preceding miniature, but here His throne floats above the floor. Although the
four apostles and four prophets are separated by the throne, they
are indistinguishable, except for the apostles' bare feet. The texts
of their banderoles are also taken from the *Te Deum (Te gloriosus
apostolorum chorus | Te prophetarum laudabilis numerus)*, while
the banderole of the Father announces, "I am alpha and omega,
God and man."

## Wednesday Hours of All Saints—Sext

65. GOD THE FATHER AND THE FOUR EVANGELIST SYMBOLS. (G–f.119)

[s] The throne of the Father, who is depicted as before, and the four
medallions with the symbols, are placed against a green background
decorated with gold patterns of stars and waves or clouds. Each of
the symbols has a scroll to identify the evengelist represented.

## Wednesday Hours of All Saints—None

66. ECCLESIASTICAL AND MILITARY SAINTS ADORE GOD THE FATHER.

[s] (G – f.120v) As before, God the Father is enthroned between two
groups: on the left are representatives of the religious orders
(Dominican, Carthusian, Franciscan, Benedictine, and one other);
on the right are five military saints in armor, of whom the foremost
is distinguished by his gold armor, blue cape, and St. George's
shield. The banderole of the Father identifies these groups as men
who have battled worldliness, while their scrolls contain two more
verses from the *Te Deum (Te per orbem terrarum . . .* and *Te
martyrum . . .)*. The Father's throne, with small clouds underneath,
hovers slightly above the floor.

## Wednesday Hours of All Saints—Vespers

67. VIRGINS ADORING GOD THE FATHER. (G – f.122)   Two groups

[s] of five virgins stand beside the throne of God, who is depicted as

in the preceding miniatures. His banderole says, "Come to me all wisest virgins," while the virgins' rolls express contempt for the world (the lay virgins on the left) and love for Christ (the nuns on the right). The throne of the Father floats on clouds above the floor.

## Wednesday Hours of All Saints—Compline

68. St. MICHAEL BATTLING A DEMON. (M – p.44) A modish Michael
[s] wrestles with an ochre demon, who claws at his armor, while being pierced by the angel's long gold cross-staff. The combat takes place on the ground, and Michael is on foot.

## Mass of All Saints

69. Sts. PETER, JOHN THE BAPTIST, AND MARTIN. (G – f.124) A full-
[s] page miniature probably preceded this scene. The three saints stand frontally with the customary attributes: Peter with keys, book, and tiara; John holding the Lamb of God on a book; and Martin in his bishop's vestments giving his cloak to a diminutive crippled beggar.

## Thursday Hours of the Holy Sacrament—Matins

70. SOLOMON DISTRIBUTING BREAD. (G – f.131) The large minia-
[s] ture beginning this series is now lacking. This scene, as the biblical quotation in the upper margin makes clear, is based on Proverbs IX, 5, in which Wisdom invites everyone to share her bread and wine, an antetype of the Eucharist. In the miniature Solomon, instead of Wisdom, and a helper dispense bread from three open sacks to three kneeling men. In the border another man walks away with a similar full sack over his shoulder. This sack and one other bear monograms; these signs may have been used for identifying grain, possibly on Catherine's estates. A banderole over Solomon has a quotation from Genesis XLVII, 13, which says that there is a want of bread in the whole world. The heads of the Apostles Andrew and Paul appear in the upper corners, and from them unroll two scrolls, one with a quotation from John VI, 9, about the multiplication of loaves and fishes, and the other from Paul's First

Epistle to the Corinthians (X, 16) on the communion bread being the body of Christ.                                                    [PLATE 19]

## Thursday Hours of the Sacrament—Prime

71. MOSES AND JOHN THE EVANGELIST KNEEL BEFORE A MONSTRANCE.
[s]  (G – f.133)   On either side of a central altar with a monstrance kneel Moses (with black horns) and John. Above each is a banderole: Moses's has a quotation from Deuteronomy VIII, 3, on the gift of manna (an antetype for the bread of the Eucharist), and John's has one from Apocalypse II, 17, on a new gift of manna. Behind Moses is a kneeling old man in contemporary dress, probably Nehemias, since the scroll in the left margin has a text from Second Esdras or Nehemias IX, 15. In the right margin is one from John VI, 35. Both texts deal with the meaning of bread.

## Thursday Hours of the Sacrament—Terce

72. COMMUNION.  (G – f.134v)   With his back to the altar, the
[s]  celebrant holds the chalice in one hand and with the other places a portion of the host in the mouth of one of the two kneeling communicants. On top of the altar is a monstrance, and in front of the gold retable are two candles. The heads of Elijah and Moses appear in the upper corners, each with a banderole. Elijah's text is taken from III Kings XIX, 6, and Moses's is from Leviticus XXII, 3. Two more quotations are written in the margins, both from John (VI, 33, and XVIII, 3).

## Thursday Hours of the Sacrament—Sext

73. ISAIAH, AARON, PAUL, AND LUKE ADORE A MONSTRANCE.  (G –
[s]  f.136)   The Old Testament figures, without halos, kneel on the left of the altar; the New Testament ones on the right. In front of Aaron is a mitre, and above his head is a banderole with a text drawn from Exodus XII, 48. A second banderole above Paul's head has a quotation from his Epistle to the Corinthians (XI, 28). Two further scrolls are unrolled in the margins with texts from Isaiah XLV, 15 (left), and Luke VIII, 17 (right).

[ 45 ]

## Thursday Hours of the Sacrament—None

74. GATHERING OF MANNA. (G – f.137v)  As manna, looking much
[s] like large hailstones, rains from heaven, Aaron and five Israelites
gather it in skirts, hats, and baskets. Moses stands at the side and
watches. He has black horns and carries a staff, and beside him is
Aaron wearing a mitre. Biblical texts in the margin, drawn from
Exodus XVI, 4, Exodus XVI, 15, John VI, 11, and Paul's Epistle
to the Corinthians XI, 24, describe and interpret the event.

## Thursday Hours of the Sacrament—Vespers

75. SUPPER AT EMMAUS. (G–f.139) Seated behind the table is Christ
[s] in pilgrim's garb with shell badges; seated in front are Luke with
a halo and Cleopas without. Christ is breaking bread; Luke reaches
for some meat; and Cleopas is drinking from a glass. In the margins
are four explanatory and exegetical texts drawn from the Bible:
Exodus XVI, 35; Lamentations of Jeremiah IV, 4; Matthew
XXVIII, 20; and Luke XXIV, 35.

## Thursday Hours of the Sacrament—Compline

76. ISRAELITES EATING THE PASSOVER LAMB AND UNLEAVENED BREAD.
[s] (G – f.140v)  Four children of Israel stand around a circular table
eating lamb and unleavened bread. In the upper left is the head
of Isaiah with a banderole text from his book (LVII, 11); in the
opposite corner are another head and text which have not been
identified, but the text reads: *Immolabit haedum multitudo
filiorum israel.* Two quotations from Paul's First Epistle to the
Corinthians (V, 7, and XI, 27) give a Christian meaning to the
Passover food, and a third Latin quotation in the upper margin
attributed to Isaiah, "the children of Israel with a lamb," provides
a title for the miniature.

## Mass of the Holy Sacrament

77. LAST SUPPER.  (G – f.142v)  Christ sits in the middle of the rec-
[L] tangular table, and the apostles, divided into two equal groups,

are arranged around the two ends of the table. John rests his head on Christ's chest, and Judas, with a small black demon by his open mouth, is being fed unleavened bread by Christ. The other apostles are eating and drinking. On the floor in the foreground, two dogs snarl over a bone, and a maid enters through the door on the right. The rather plain rectangular room is given a more formal, even liturgical, appearance by two concave niches flanking Christ in the side walls and a tall window in the end wall behind Christ's head. The significance of the scene is interpreted by two scrolls in the margins with two biblical quotations: one from Psalms (LXXVII, 25) that speaks of eating the bread of angels, and one from Luke (XIV, 15) that says, "Blessed is he that shall eat bread in the kingdom of God." [PLATE 20]

78. MOSES AND PAUL OBSERVE THE CELEBRATION OF MASS. (G–f.143)
[s] A priest kneels before an altar on which are a monstrance, a covered chalice, a book, a lectern, and two candles. Behind him stand Moses and Paul, each with a banderole. That of Moses has a quotation from Exodus (XIX, 22) in which the Lord demands the sanctification of the priests; the quotation of Paul's scroll is taken from his First Epistle to the Corinthians (XI, 31) where he speaks about judging the worthiness of those who eat the bread or drink the wine of the Eucharist. Largely hidden by Moses is another, as yet unidentified, saint.

## Friday Hours of the Compassion of God—Matins

79. DYING ADAM DISPATCHES SETH TO PARADISE. (M – p.75) This
[s] unusual cycle depicting the legend of the cross should begin with a large miniature, probably of the Tree of Knowledge or the Fall of Man, but now it starts with Adam's commanding Seth to fetch a branch of the Tree of Mercy. The cadaverous Adam lies on his deathbed and speaks to his third son, who stands beside the bed and respectfully removes his straw hat. Seth appears a second time leaving the bedside with his hat on and a staff over his shoulder— an unusual example in this manuscript of "continuous narrative." In addition to the imposing bed, the furnishings of the flatly

[ 47 ]

barrel-vaulted room include a chair beside the bed and a flameless candle resting on a small scroll in a niche above the head of the bed. A small landscape with a tree (symbolic of the Tree of Mercy?) may be seen through the window in the rear wall separating the two Seths. In the lower border are a dragon and lion rampant.

## Friday Hours of the Compassion—Lauds

80. ARCHANGEL MICHAEL GIVES SETH A BRANCH OF THE TREE OF MERCY.
[s] (M – p.85)   The archangel, having just emerged from the golden gate of Paradise, gives a branch to Seth. The two stand in front of the mauve-rose wall and gothic gatehouse of Paradise. Over the wall may be seen two trees, and through a low arched opening in the wall with a gold-barred sluice gate and a white animal (a dog?) carved above the keystone, runs water from one or all of the four rivers arising in Paradise. In the lower border, Seth's older brothers, Abel and Cain, place their offerings to God on an altar.

## Friday Hours of the Compassion—Prime

81. SETH PLANTS THE BRANCH IN THE MOUTH OF THE DEAD ADAM.
[s] (M – p.91)   The corpse of Adam, wrapped in a white shroud, has been laid out on a hillside in a cool and green landscape. Seth bends over the body and places the branch from Paradise in Adam's mouth. A seated woman with a straw hat milks a cow into a wooden pail in the lower border.

## Friday Hours of the Compassion—Terce

82. TREE GROWING FROM ADAM'S GRAVE.   (M – p.97)   The tree has
[s] grown up through a crack in the mauve-rose grave slab which is decorated with a column carved in relief. Adam's skull lies on top of the slab beside the tree, and part of his skeleton can be seen beneath the slab. A small green rodent-shaped animal is about to enter the grave, and in his lair behind a wolf-like animal chews on a bone. The green foreground is silhouetted against an orange sunset sky. In the lower border the hand of God stays the sword of Abraham about to kill his son Isaac before a flaming altar.

## Friday Hours of the Compassion—Sext

83. SOLOMON ORDERS THE TREE TO BE CUT DOWN. (M – p.101)
[s] Hoping to use the tree as a timber for his temple, Solomon commands that it be chopped down. The king and three members of his retinue stand at the right; Solomon touches the tree with his sceptre; a carpenter at the left begins to fell the tree with his axe. The scene takes place in a space enclosed by a woven fence. In the lower border a round-faced moronic boy turns two animals, probably lambs or chickens, on an open-air spit with a fire behind and dripping-pan and ladle beneath.

## Friday Hours of the Compassion—None

84. MEASURING THE TIMBER. (M – p.105) Having cut the tree and
[s] shaped the timber, the carpenter is measuring it with a piece of string under the eyes of Solomon and two members of his retinue. The axe blade has been buried in the stump of the tree in the foreground; the enclosing woven fence has disappeared. A yellow and green "dragon" in the lower border is being ridden by a harp-playing dwarf (?).

## Friday Hours of the Compassion—Vespers

85. QUEEN OF SHEBA FORDING A STREAM (THE KEDRON ?). (M–p.109)
[s] When Solomon's carpenters found that they could not use the timber for the temple, because it was always too long or too short, they built a foot-bridge from it. The Queen of Sheba, recognizing that it was the wood upon which Christ would be crucified, refused to step on it and, according to one of the many versions of the story, waded through the stream. She is shown here holding up her long dress and fording the stream, while Solomon and one of his courtiers watch from the right bank, and, on the left bank, a negro attendant of the queen, exotically dressed in gold and purple, shows a piece of jewelry to a lady of Solomon's court. The foot-bridge, made of the single timber and a rough log railing, is visible behind the queen. This scene, especially in light of the following miniature, probably represents the curing of the queen's mal-

formation, duck feet, through the power of the Tree of Mercy. The border contains a woman spinning and displaying her garden produce before a conically tented market booth.          [PLATE 21]

## Friday Hours of the Compassion—Compline

86. MIRACLES OF THE POOL OF BETHESDA. (M – p.114)   The pool
[S] is mentioned in the fifth chapter of John's Gospel, and its healing powers are attributed to an angel who occasionally stirs its waters. These powers were also explained later, in the Middle Ages, by the presence of the wood of the Tree of Mercy in the pool, which welled up over the spot where Solomon had fearfully buried the wood upon which, according to prediction, the kingdom of the Jews would end. In this scene the angel stirs the water and the log, not the timber, floats in the pool. One lame man sits by the pool holding a staff; another lies beside the pool; and a third is being lowered into the water by an attendant. In the lower border, Christ kneels on the ground and washes the feet of Peter.          [PLATE 22]

## Mass of the Cross

87. CHRIST STANDING ON THE LOWERED CROSS. (M – p.121)   A sec-
[S] ond full-page miniature missing from this series about the cross must have faced this scene. Christ, bleeding from the wounds of His flagellation and crucifixion, stands in triumph with one foot on the reclining cross. He is dressed only in a loin cloth and wears His crown of thorns. There are no other figures, and in the barren landscape there is no human habitation. The scene is symbolic or allegorical, rather than historical. Another allegorical scene appears in the lower border, Christ in the Winepress; He holds two whips from the flagellation under His arms, and the blood from His wounds runs through a trough into a golden chalice below.

## Saturday Hours of the Virgin—Matins

88. CREATION OF EVE. (M – p.138)   A very blond Creator, dressed
[L] in lavender and rose robes, blesses and touches the hands of Eve, who emerges half-length from behind, not from the side of, Adam.

He in turn looks up at God, his hand supporting the back of his head, but his body is turned away from Him. Like their Creator, both Adam and Eve are extremely blond. The three figures are silhouetted against a dark blue-green hillock on which grow five trees; two of these are orange trees, and one appears to be a palm. The border is composed of spreading leaves and fleshy buds.

89. EVE AND THE VIRGIN. (M – p.139)  The two Eves, the original
[s] Eve and the new Eve, stand on opposite sides of the Tree of Knowledge, from which the serpent hands a piece of fruit to the first Eve. She is naked, except for the leaf with which she covers herself, but the Virgin is heavily clothed from head to foot, as is the infant Jesus whom she holds. This opposition is made explicit by the banderole held above the tree by an angel: *Auctrix peccati Eva, Auctrix meriti Maria.* The highly symmetrical border forms a bower of leaves and flowers.

## Saturday Hours of the Virgin—Prime

90. TREE OF JESSE. (M – p.148)  From Isaiah's mention of Jesse's
[s] root, its branch *(virga)*, and its flower, and from the genealogies of Christ given in the Gospels, the Middle Ages created a family tree arising in Jesse, continuing through Christ's ancestors, and concluding with the Virgin and Her Son. Here the tree grows from the chest of Jesse who lies upon a pallet on the ground; among the leaves are distributed twelve unidentifiable bust "portraits" of the royal ancestors, arranged without regard for their generations; and seated at the top is the Virgin with an open book on Her lap. David plays his harp under the tree, but Christ is absent from the scene. The border is composed of large multicolor and fanciful leaves.

## Saturday Hours of the Virgin—Terce

91. JOACHIM AND ANNE: THE IMMACULATE CONCEPTION. (M–p.145)
[s] What appears to be a double portrait of the Virgin's parents is actually a rare version of the Immaculate Conception. Joachim and Anne stand upon a floor with tiles of the sun and moon and

against a burnished gold ground. He holds a scroll with a latin legend saying that Anne will give birth to the mother of the Saviour; she holds a book and gestures in demure surprise, as her daughter does in the Annunciation. Above, in the blue arc of heaven, God appears holding a gold globe and blessing Anne; from Him radiate golden rays toward the abdomen of Anne. Around the page is a border of fantastic leaves of uterine shape enclosing a gold bar.

## Saturday Hours of the Virgin—Sext

92. HOLY FAMILY AT WORK. (M–p.149) Within a domestic interior,
[s] the Virgin is seated at a loom weaving; Joseph stands while planing a board; and the Infant practices His first steps in a walker. Many homely furnishings and utensils are distributed through the room: a shelf of silver or pewter plate, a cabinet of weaving materials, a fireplace with an adjustable hook for holding pots, a carpenter's bench and various tools, etc. Two windows open onto the landscape beyond. The infant Jesus holds a banderole that floats up toward His mother; its Latin legend says, "I am your solace." The border is composed of small delicate leaves and flowers.

[PLATE 23]

## Saturday Hours of the Virgin—None

93. HOLY FAMILY AT SUPPER. (M–p.151) The Virgin sits upon a
[s] yellow mat on the floor nursing the infant Jesus, and Joseph rests in a barrel chair spooning his soup. The room is not the same as that of the preceding miniature, but it has a similar abundance of furnishings and utensils. In the tall cylindrical fireplace, two pots are cooking, one in the fire and one hanging over the flames from an adjustable hook; tongs lean against the side; a hand grill hangs above; and a hook, ledge, and warming niche are to be seen. Beside the fireplace are a shelf of silver or pewter plate, a pair of shears, a bellows, a wooden cabinet with food and various dishes, and a basket with herbs (?). On the side wall is a rack with still other utensils. The leaves and flowers of the border are unusually delicate.

[PLATE 2]

## Saturday Hours of the Virgin—Vespers

94. ASCENSION. (M – p.153)  Unlike the usual crowded Ascension,
[s] this scene is limited to the devout kneeling Virgin who looks up
at Her Son disappearing into the clouds, only His feet and the bottom of His garment still visible. This scene of private devotion
takes place by the door of a small church-like building. The border
comprises small leaves and flowers.

## Saturday Hours of the Virgin—Compline

95. FUNERAL PROCESSION OF THE VIRGIN. (M – p.157)  The funeral
[s] cortege consists of the twelve apostles: John, carrying a palm, leads
the way; behind him is the coffin covered with gold cloth and
carried by four of the apostles; beside the coffin are Peter, who
sprinkles holy water on it, and Paul, who censes it; the remaining
five apostles follow behind. Beyond a small hillock stands the
priest Jephonias with a group of soldiers; two other soldiers, in
order to turn back the procession, have put their hands on the
coffin, but their hands have stuck miraculously to it—indeed one's
hand has broken off at the wrist. Small leaves and flowers compose
the border.

## Saturday Mass of the Virgin

96. CRUCIFIX WITH GOD THE FATHER, THE VIRGIN, A BISHOP SAINT,
[L] AND CATHERINE OF CLEVES. (M – p.160)  The sense of this devotional scene is explained by the spoken words on banderoles:
Catherine pleads with the Holy Mother of God to pray for her;
the Virgin intercedes with Her Son to be gracious to Catherine on
account of the breasts which nursed Him; Christ asks, in the name
of His wounds, for His Father to spare Catherine; and the Father
tells His Son, "Your prayer has been heard with favor." On the
tile floor, at either side of the cross, kneel the Virgin (on a red
carpet) and Catherine (on a blue carpet). The Virgin, one of Her
breasts bare and spurting milk, looks up to Her Son; Catherine looks
down at her praying hands and carries over her arm the rosary
that is shown almost actual size in one of the manuscript's borders

(no. 116). She wears a mauve-rose ermine-lined houppelande, and her hair is worn in pointed templers under a goffered veil, identical with that of the personification of piety in no. 57 and similar to that of her portrait in no. 1. (Margaret Van Eyck has the same coiffure in the portrait painted by her husband Jan in 1439.) On the floor in front of her are a tiny poodle-like dog and a beautifully painted stool with a half-open book. Behind her stands an unidentified bishop saint with a crozier, presumably her patron saint, who gently touches her shoulder with his gloved hand. The Christ is not dead, but rather looks up beseechingly to His Father who appears in the corner surrounded by angels, wearing a tiara, holding a globe, and blessing His Son. The miniature is surrounded by an elaborate pattern of orange interlace knots on which are hung panels of geometrical intarsia work which look Italian or Spanish.

[PLATE 24]

97. VIRGIN AND CHILD IN A GRAPE ARBOR. (M – p.161) The Virgin,
[s] wearing a gold crown and reading, is seated on the grass and surrounded by a low brick wall upon which is erected a gold latticework with grape vines. The infant Jesus and two angels collect bunches of grapes from the arbor, a clear reference to the Crucifixion and the Eucharist. Over the Virgin's head, a third angel holds a banderole with the introit of the Mass below: *Salve sancta parens enixa puerpera regem.* Most of the border is composed of textiles and lacework, but at the bottom are six singing angels standing around a lectern and enclosed by a large throne with pillows carrying an armorial design resembling the Cleves device.

[PLATE 25]

## Penitential Psalms

98. MAN OF SORROWS WITH KNEELING FRANCISCANS. (G – f.151)
[s] The Penitential Psalms may have opened originally with a full-page miniature; if so, it is now missing. With His wounds showing, wearing the crown of thorns, and holding the two whips of the flagellation, Christ stands half-length in His tomb and in front of an orange and green cloth that hangs from the arms of the cross behind. At the sides of the tomb are two groups of four kneeling

[ 54 ]

Franciscans; each group has a banderole, and though both legends are only partly legible, they ask for forgiveness of sins. In the lower border is the reclining Lamb of God holding the staff and banner of the Resurrection and spurting blood from His chest into a nearby chalice.

## Office of the Dead

99. MOUTH OF HELL. (G – f.168v) Not one, but three mouths are
[L] incorporated into this awesome vision of the castellated gate of Hell. At the top of the structure is a blue-green head whose lower part is transformed into stone architecture, its mouth forming an ogive arch enclosing a rectangular window that opens into the fiery interior, and its lower jaw forming a crenelated parapet from which two demons throw stones onto the sinners below. The skull-decorated facade is flanked by two towers that are actually cylindrical furnaces whose fires heat two cauldrons at the top. Into these cauldrons, demons are casting sinners that they have clawed and hacked. The mouth below is actually two, one inside the other. The outer head, with gold eyes and flames from its nostrils, has its yellow-lined lips pulled wide, and attached to each point of the scalloped edge is a crab-like claw. Within the circular opening of the jaws and teeth of the outer mouth is the crimson inner head with its gold eyes and gaping toothless mouth, in which souls are being boiled in a vat by demons. Outside the mouth, many more souls are being tormented: one group chained to a wheelbarrow is brought up by a demon; another chained group is being dragged into the flames; still another group, caught in a flaming cavern below the ground, is being prodded with a spear; and many separate souls are pulled, clawed, hammered, speared, and devoured. The kinds of demons are as varied as their tortures—they are black, red, green, and blue; some are hairy; some have claws; some have quills; some look like frogs, some like pigs, some like insects, and some look like no beast of this world. In the violence of its imagery, this painting anticipates the works of Hieronymous Bosch. Out of the mouth of a green demon in the lower border come scrolls listing the seven deadly sins. [PLATE 26]

100. FUNERAL. (G – f.169) From a chapel or church, whose vaulting
[s] can be seen through a doorway, and where the Office or Mass for
the Dead has just been concluded, the mourners enter another
room and approach the coffin. They are dressed entirely in black,
but for their white pattens. The coffin is covered by a black cloth
with two long strips of gold forming a cross on the top. Three gold
candlesticks with burning tapers are placed on the coffin, and
behind it stand three clerics, one holding a cross-staff, another
sprinkling holy water and reading, and a third filling his censer.
They are garbed in surplices; each has a black amice and a black
maniple; and the central figure has a black stole. In the border,
two dragons hold a golden basket of apples between them.

## Suffrages

101. ST. MICHAEL BATTLING DEMONS. (M – p.204) The manuscript's
[s] remaining miniatures, mostly "portraits" of individual saints, illustrate an unusually long series of suffrages, brief devotions usually
dedicated to a single saint. They begin with St. Michael standing
triumphantly on the bodies of two demons and raising his sword
over a third, cowering, demon. A green crown on his head, the
saint is dressed in a pale purple cassock, a green stole, and a long
red mantle that has slipped down from his shoulders. The battle
takes place among rocks with flaming fissures, in one of which
another demon can be seen.

102. GUARDIAN ANGEL AND DEMON BATTLE OVER A CORPSE. (M–p.206)
[s] The corpse, its winding sheet partly unwound, is laid out in a
coffin of which one side and the top have been removed. Its guardian angel, modishly dressed, wields a sword and struggles with a
brown, winged demon over a large, blank-page, gilt-edged book.
The coffin is placed on a wooden rack beside a grave, which is being
dug by a man with a long-handled shovel. A pick and spade are
in the grave. Below, in the border, a seated female mourner wrings
her hands; apparently she is the widow of no. 41, who also seems
to appear in the borders of nos. 107 and 109.

103. St. JOHN BAPTIST. (M – p.208) In a wilderness landscape of
[s] rocks and caves and against an orange sunset sky, the saint stands
holding the bannered staff of the Resurrection and pointing to
the wounded Lamb of God held in his arm. His body and face are
gaunt, and his hands are red and raw. He wears a mauve-rose cloak
over a robe of golden skin.

104. St. PETER APOSTLE. (M – p.210) For most of the miniatures illus-
[s] trating the suffrages a standard format is used, consisting of a standing "portrait" of the saint and a simple stage set of a tiled floor
and a textile backdrop, but within this format there is a ceaseless
variation of color and pattern. Important as these variations are,
the setting will only be described when it is exceptional in some
way or interesting in iconography. Here Peter carries his attributes,
keys and a book, and wears priestly vestments, a plain mauve-rose
cope over surplice, dalmatic, and green stole. In the border are
three entwined fish painted with silver; they are, of course, attributes of the fisherman Peter, fisher of fish and of men.

105. St. PAUL APOSTLE. (M – p.213) Unlike the priestly Peter, Paul
[s] is dressed in a long blue gown under a long crimson cape. He has
his own attributes, a sword and a book. A small King David
wrestles a lion in the lower border. The exact reason for juxtapos-
ing David and Paul is not clear, although there are obvious paral-
lels between the two, and Paul is sometimes depicted with lions.

106. SAINT ANDREW APOSTLE. (M – p.214) Wearing the normal
[s] apostle's garb, long cape and long gown, Andrew stands holding
his X-shaped cross. Contained in the border is a small scene of a
hairy wildman slitting the throat of a white goose or swan, a theme
which has no discernible connection with Andrew, nor is it clearly
antithetical to him.

107. St. JAMES MAJOR. (M – p.216) The saint stands in a landscape
[s] between two hills topped by castles. He wears the apostle's cape
and gown and a broad-brimmed pilgrim's hat decorated with a shell.
With pilgrim's pouch at his side, he carries a large pilgrim's staff
and a book bound in a loose envelope-binding (*Hülleneinband*).

[ 57 ]

At the bottom of the page, a weeping woman dressed in black is comforted by a cleric (?), caped and hooded in white, to whom she gives something, probably money. These figures appear to be the same two seen in front of the deathbed in miniature no. 41, and she is also in the border of no. 102. It is likely that the grieving widow is about to leave on a pilgrimage, possibly to Compostela, for she appears on the road in the border of no. 109.

108. St. john evangelist. (M – p.218) The youthful saint holds in
[s] his left hand the poison cup, shaped like a chalice with a black demon in its bowl, and blesses with his other hand. His martyrdom is shown in the lower border: with his hands in prayer, he squats in a cauldron of oil under which is a fire of logs.

109. St. thomas apostle. (M – p.221) Thomas supports a lance
[s] and holds a book in an envelope-binding. Below, in the border, a female pilgrim walks along with two rectangular packs strapped over her shoulders and with a white drum-shaped "crown" bearing an illegible inscription. She appears to be the woman of nos. 41, 102, and 107, and is probably joined with St. Thomas, because of his far-reaching travels.

110. St. james minor. (M – p.224) A pedum staff and a short string
[s] of beads are held by the saint. At the open-air wine stand below, one man fills a pitcher from a cask, while another approaches carrying a branch with grape(?) leaves and an empty tankard. The drinking scene is the antithesis of St. James who was famous for his abstinence.

111. St. philip apostle. (M – p.226) From among his attributes the
[s] saint bears a book and cross-staff; he stands before an unusually rich textile of yellow-green and gold patterns over a blue-green background. Three figures in the margin are baking: a woman measures the ingredients; one man kneads the dough and forms the small round cakes, and a second puts the cakes into a fiery stone or brick oven. Philip was often considered the patron of pastry-cooks. [plate 27]

112. St. Bartholomew apostle. (M – p.228) The saint, a large
[s] knife in his hand, is painted against a gold-patterned blue-green
textile. Around the page is a border of pretzels and biscuits; these
seem to have no eucharistic significance, although pretzels are
sometimes found on the table of the Last Supper. The biscuits look
somewhat like hosts, but lack the cross marking used in this book
for the eucharistic wafer. Instead, they relate either to the preceding scene of secular baking, or to some special patronage of
Bartholomew.                                         [PLATE 28]

113. St. Matthew apostle. (M – p.231) The saint carries a book
[s] and a carpenter's square; the square attribute is unusual and as yet
unexplained, but it connects Matthew with wood-working, as does
the border, a simulated wooden frame of carved rosettes, vines,
and leaves. Running around the four corners is a gold inscription
telling why Matthew, as one of the Evangelists, was assigned the
form of a man for his symbol; it begins: *Formam viri datam
matheo. . . .*

114. St. Simon apostle. (M – p.233) In a setting of unusual refine-
[s] ment, the saint stands holding his attributes, a book from which he
reads and a long-bladed saw. The border is composed of fish nets,
one of which is being repaired by a man leaning out from behind
the miniature. Simon is rarely connected with fishing; perhaps it is
from a confusion with Simon Peter.

115. St. Matthias apostle. (M – p.235) The saint holding his at-
[s] tributes, a book and a short-handled axe, wears a white turban,
a yellow tunic, and a crimson mantle. In the border are three
swastikas, each composed of four Matthias axes.

116. Adoration of the Magi. (M – p.237) This narrative scene,
[s] which interrupts the series of hagiological portraits, precedes the
suffrage for the Three Kings. With no sign of their entourage, the
kings approach from the right; they are expensively and fashionably dressed, and each carries a gold ciborium-like vessel. The first
king, his tall crowned hat on the ground before him, kneels in
front of the Child and offers Him gold; the second king points to

the distant star; and the third and youngest stands waiting his turn. The plainly dressed Virgin sits at the entry to the stable holding Her Infant on Her knees; behind Her, inside the stable, sits a stolid and rather plebeian Joseph, his hands upon his staff, and beside him are the unruly ass and an ox eating from the manger. In the distance is a cool green landscape with a village, a windmill, and castles. Disposed around the page is Catherine of Cleves's red-beaded rosary, which ends in tassels with gold and pearls. Attached to it are a seven-pointed star of pearls and gold, a small cross of the same materials, and a blue purse with draw strings, a gold mouth, three red tassels drawn through pearls, and with the letters CD in gold encrusted with pearls *(Catherina Duxissa?).* [PLATE 29]

117. St. gregory the great. (M – p.240) Holding a cross-staff and
[s] a book and wearing his papal tiara, the saint stands before a crimson textile. A single row of twenty-five gold and silver coins forms the border. Painted with remarkable care, these coins seem to reproduce contemporary money, and, although the coins are represented as showing some wear, their designs are clear, and a few of their inscriptions can be read. Two or three have DUX: ARNOLD': GLE, presumably the husband of Catherine of Cleves, but some of the silver coins seem to be Burgundian. These marginal subjects may have no immediate connection with St. Gregory, but he was one of the great administrators of the church.

118. St. jerome. (M–p.242) Dressed in his crimson cardinal's robes
[s] and hat, Jerome holds a book, while he reaches down to remove a thorn from the paw of a lion beside him. The page is a *trompe l'oeil* in which the text and miniature appear to be part of a large processional banner of patterned mauve-rose silk, which hangs from a cross-arm terminated by two human hands holding little bells. The cross-arm was probably supported on a staff of which only the gold cross head is visible.

119. St. ambrose. (M–p.244) Wearing a surplice, cope, and mitre,
[s] Ambrose holds his bishop's crozier and a book. The border is formed of eleven mussels, open and with their inner tissues painted gold. They are represented with great precision and are arranged

like a necklace for which the crab in the lower border forms the clasp. These animals are not part of St. Ambrose's iconography.

[PLATE 30]

120. St. AUGUSTINE. (M – p.245) Except for the heart pierced by
[s] two arrows that Augustine holds, he is depicted much as St. Ambrose. The border consists of four pieces of chain held at the corners by two angels and two golden-eyed demons; the chains run through or are attached to four hearts like, but larger than, the one held by the saint; blank banderoles, some gold and some white and brown, spiral around the remaining chain.

121. Sts. CORNELIUS AND CYPRIAN. (M – p.247) Associated in the
[s] liturgy, these two saints stand side by side in a double portrait. Each has his appropriate attributes: Cornelius has a curved golden horn, the papal cross-staff, and tiara; Cyprian holds a sword and crozier and wears his bishop's mitre. A collection of bird cages and training cages comprise the border. There are five cages of differing shapes and decoration, one bird perch, and two training devices, one a long spiraling cage to discourage flight and the other a revolving drum, perhaps for the same purpose. On one of the elaborate cloth cage covers are the letters C and D plus a third letter that may possibly be a G. (See no. 116.) These bird cages may only reflect an interest of Catherine of Cleves, but St. Cornelius was usually considered the patron of domestic animals.     [PLATE 31]

122. St. ANTHONY. (M – p.249) With his pig at his feet, Anthony
[s] stands beside a small salmon-colored building in a verdant landscape. He is dressed in a white surplice, pale lavender dalmatic (?), and black hooded cape; he holds an open book in one hand, from which he reads, and a cane and bell in the other. The pig and the building also have bells. In the middle distance is an enclosure surrounded by a woven fence and a gate with gateposts formed of two living trees, whose stripped branches form a perfect arch above. The border simulates stone, and its carved leaves are painted various colors.

123. Sts. FABIAN AND SEBASTIAN. (M – p.253) This double portrait
[s] is placed in the usual surroundings of tiled floor and textile back-

drop. Pope Fabian is dressed as other pontiffs, but holds a sword as well as the papal staff. The upper part of Sebastian's body is naked and pierced by many arrows; the lower part is covered by a loin cloth and long red hose; his wrists are tied around a mauve-rose column, like that of Christ's Flagellation. Distributed in the borders surrounding the text are different kinds of archery equipment: cross-bows, long bows with both one and two strings, arrows and bolts, and quivers and bolt pouches. Obviously these are related to Sebastian's martyrdom.

124. CONVERSION OF ST. HUBERT. (M – p.256) The saint, wearing a
[s] gray hat with a high turned-up brim and with two feathers, one crimson and one white, and dressed in a crimson and white gown, slit front and back, sits astride a long-legged short-bodied gray horse. They have just stopped suddenly, for Hubert is still pulling back on the reins. Before him is a miraculous vision, a crucifix between the antlers of a deer that rears up and crosses its forelegs. Below the deer, the first of the saint's three hunting dogs sits on its back haunches and raises its forepaws in prayer. This is an early example of the Conversion and is unusual in many of its details. Contained in the border is a small scene of a fawn attacked by an eagle. A lost leaf with a portrait of St. Quirinus once followed this page.

125. MARTYRDOM OF ST. ERASMUS. (M – p.258) Naked except for
[s] his loincloth and mitre, Erasmus is tied to a wooden pallet raised a few inches off the ground by two low "sawhorses." His intestines are being wound from an incision in his abdomen onto a wooden spindle being rotated by two spoked wheels that are turned by two executioners. The scene takes place in a rather bare landscape. In the border is a small boy wearing a conical hat and a collar of long radiating sticks; he is riding a hobby-horse.

126. TEN THOUSAND MARTYRS AND ST. ACACIUS. (M – p.262) The
[s] legend of the martyrdom of the Roman centurion and his 10,000 legionnaires on Mount Ararat has been transformed here into a scene of ten men, naked except for loincloths and crowns of thorns, spitted on the spiny branches of three bare trees (because of a confusion of the centurion's name with the acacia tree). Standing

beside the trees is Acacius transformed into a bishop, probably through confusion with one of the bishop-saints of the same name; he carries a crozier and wears a mitre and other pontifical vestments. At the feet of the saint are three tiny lions, two of which lick his feet, a puzzling detail. Around the edge of the page is a banderole with an abridgement of the Apostles' Creed winding between portraits of the Apostles set in small white flowers.

127. ST. BLAISE.   (M – p.264)   Dressed in a bishop's vestments, includ-
[s] ing mitre and crozier, the saint holds over his shoulder a long-tined wool comb, the instrument of his marytrdom. The textile behind him has a motif of ferocious animals chained together, a reference no doubt to his legendary triumphs over wild beasts. Sometimes St. Blaise is shown with the birds that brought him food, but they do not appear here; instead, an antithesis is shown—a monkey leans out of the border of spiraling leaves and steals birds from a nest within the initial O.

128. ST. LAWRENCE.   (M – p.266)   Vested as a deacon, Lawrence holds
[s] a book, a purse, and the instrument of his martyrdom, a gridiron. Some of the floor tiles have a design of two biting fish, a motif that is elaborated in the border of fish eating fish. Although fish and fishing do not belong to the legend or patronage of Lawrence, he was the patron of the poor, as his purse here testifies, and the proverbial eating of the little fish by the big, a literary and pictorial theme of great popularity in the fifteenth and sixteenth century, was an allegory of the poor being eaten by the rich. That men, like fish, eat fish is implied by the fishlines and hooks which have already caught some of the fish at the bottom of the page. Many of these fish are painted with silver to imitate the iridescence of their scales.                                              [PLATE 32]

129. ST. VINCENT.   (M – p.268)   Wearing his deacon's vestments, the
[s] saint holds his attributes, a book and a rod with three hooks. As Vincent was the patron of wine-growers, the border consists of a grape vine. Upon this vine are several different kinds of butterflies and moths, executed with great care and in much detail; perhaps these species are pests to viniculture, since some of them do seem to attack the vine.

130. ST. VALENTINE. (M – p.269)  Dressed in a deacon's dalmatic
[s] (with the names of Jesus and Mary in gold) rather than in a bishop's vestments, as he usually is, the saint holds a book and a sword, the means of his martyrdom. At the bottom of the border, composed of feather-like leaves and delicate rose and crimson flowers, are two dragonflies devouring a fly or a bee; this subject may be explained by Valentine's patronage of the beekeepers.

131. LAPIDATION OF ST. STEPHEN. (M – p.271)  Already struck by
[s] one stone, Stephen begins to fall, as he is being blessed by Christ from an arc of heaven above. There are four executioners: one raises a large rock over his head; another reaches back to throw one stone while holding a second one in his other hand; a third lies awkwardly on the ground, though about to throw a stone; a fourth removes his jacket which he will give to Saul (the future St. Paul), who already holds the jacket of one executioner. Stephen is dressed in his deacon's dalmatic. In the lower border a man attacks an advancing boar with a spear; the reference of this scene to Stephen is not clear.

132. ST. GEORGE KILLING THE DRAGON. (M – p.272)  The knightly
[s] saint, wearing gilded body armor and a large wide hat to which are attached a red and a white feather, holds a shield with the cross of St. George and sits in a saddle with long steel leg-shields reaching down to the stirrup. His horse is richly caparisoned and wears a steel poitrel and a red-lined white cloth over its hindquarters. The dragon, impaled by the saint's lance, has a yellow-bellied, lizard-like body. On a hillock behind kneels the princess, praying and holding the leash of a small white lamb, and in the distance is a walled city. A virgin, in the border, holds in her lap the golden horn of a submissive unicorn that sits on its haunches beside her; the virgin and unicorn parallel the princess and the lamb, and both refer to the Virgin and her Son.

133. ST. CHRISTOPHER CARRYING THE INFANT CHRIST. (M – p.275)
[s] Christopher, a veritable giant, balances himself with a long staff while he makes his way precariously to the shore; on his shoulder he carries a small Christ, who holds a golden globe and blesses the

[ 64 ]

saint. The landscape is almost sur-real; the water is like glass reflecting the cliffs and the distant fishermen standing in their boat; its surface is broken by a few ripples in the foreground and by the radiating wavelets made by a jumping fish in the background; a few ducks, almost microscopic in scale, float among reeds in the far distance; the orange sunset sky grades off into a deep blue night sky with gold stars and moon. On a ledge in the cliffs at one side the usual hermit lights the saint's way ineffectually with a lantern. In the lower border, a man pushes and pulls at the gateway in which he stands; this is probably Samson knocking down the gates of Gaza before carrying them off, a conventional parallel for Christopher.

134. St. Hadrian. (M–p.277) A modish soldier wearing plate armor,
[s] one side crimson and the other blue, and a tall hat with two white feathers, Hadrian holds the instruments of his martyrdom, a sword and an anvil. White bands of his rose-colored cape carry a long illegible inscription. In the lower border three animals, probably griffins, put their jaws together in such a way as to give the illusion of a single fang-filled mouth.

135. St. Martin dividing his cloak with a beggar. (M – p.279)
[s] The young and fashionably dressed saint turns in his saddle and cuts off a large piece of his cloak, the end of which is already draped over the head and shoulders of a scabby beggar standing with the aid of a crutch and a wooden leg. A second crippled beggar sits in the roadway reaching up with his begging bowl. In the sky above appears Christ holding the piece cut from the saint's cloak; a blank banderole unrolls from His face. The scene is set at a gate of Amiens, through which Martin has just come. The border of the page is composed of oblong gold cards, engraved with geometrical designs and, in two instances, with the names of Jesus or Mary; these cards, which may have been used for some special devotions, possibly connected with St. Martin, are linked together by blank scrolls that run through slots in the cards.

136. St. Nicholas. (M – p.280) Although garbed in his episcopal
[s] vestments, crozier, mitre, chasuble, gloves, etc., the saint carries no

special attributes and merely blesses with his right hand. This omission, surprising in a saint with so many attributes, may be explained by the unusual border. The outermost band around the page is plain vellum that is very delicately painted on its inner undulating edge to simulate clouds which appear to open up to a calm deep-blue sky with gold stars surrounding the text and miniature. This opening in the clouds is an extraordinarily realistic, yet emblematic, representation of Nicholas's miraculous calming of a storm at sea, an act that made him the patron of seafarers. In each of the four corners of the starry sky are three monstrous moon faces, each of a different color (black, orange, or green) and each with a silver crescent around its moon face; in the center of each group is a golden ball into which the monsters sink their teeth and over which they seem to struggle, each trying to push the others away with rudimentary arms and hands. Golden balls, sometimes depicted as golden apples, are a common attribute of Nicholas, symbolic of the gifts of gold he made to three young women to provide them with dowries and to save them from prostitution. Normally three in number, these golden balls became the emblem of pawnbrokers, of whom Nicholas was the patron saint. It is thus possible that the monsters are meant to be pawnbrokers; certainly they represent some kind of greed.

137. St. benedict. (M – p.283) The saint, silhouetted against a
[s] splendid crimson textile and blue and brown tiles, is garbed in the black Benedictine habit and holds a book and an abbot's crozier. In the blue floor-tiles are some letters, usually PI and once a G or B, but they are too small to read confidently. If they are unrelated to the saint, as seems likely, are they connected with Catherine or the artist? Below, Benedict's drowning disciple Placidus is rescued by St. Maurus, who walks on the water following St. Benedict's instructions.

138. St. servatius. (M – p.284) He is depicted as the Bishop of
[s] Tongres, a city in northeastern Belgium whence his cult spread into neighboring regions. Besides a crozier he holds two silver keys given him by St. Peter, according to legend. In the lower border two dragons with entwined necks and biting a golden object may

refer, if they are not mere decoration, to the dragon driven out of the country by the saint.

139. ST. BERNARD. (M – p.286) Instead of the proper white garb of
[S] the Cistercians, the saint wears a brown cassock and holds an abbot's crozier and a book. Around the page is a kind of chaplet of plumes (?) linked by interlaced knots of gold bands, the significance of which has not been determined. At a small gap between two plumes is the bust of a praying monk, apparently dressed as Bernard, but without a halo; a gold crown is being placed on the figure's head by a hand which reaches down from one of the plumes. This is conceivably William of Aquitaine, who was erroneously thought to have become a hermit to expiate for his sins and the excommunication from which St. Bernard saved him. If so, the hand would be the church returning his crown.

140. ST. THOMAS AQUINAS. (M – p.287) Holding no attributes other
[L] than an open book that he reads, the rotund saint is garbed in the Dominican habit, except that his black cape is covered with gold stars, a motif derived presumably from the vision of Albertus Manducasinus of Brescia, and an allusion perhaps to his being called *Doctor angelicus*. A pouch, a case, and keys hang from his girdle.

141. ST. LEONARD. (M – p.288) Represented as an abbot, Leonard
[S] carries attributes of a crozier, a book, and fetters.

142. ST. ALEXIS. (M – p.290) This patron of pilgrims and beggars
[S] is dressed plainly but well in a lavender houppelande and a mauve-rose cape, although he is barefoot. He holds only a ladder, his most common attribute, and stands before a striking textile of crimson on green. In the lower border he is shown dead upon a bed in his cubicle beneath the ladder-like stairs of his parents' house, clasping a scroll. According to legend, after giving away all of his wealth and making a pilgrimage to the Holy Land, he lived under the stairs of his parents' house, unrecognized. He was identified after his death by the letter clutched in his hands and released only after the benediction of Pope Boniface I.

143. HOLY FAMILY: ST. ANNE, VIRGIN, AND CHILD.  (M – p.292)
[s] St. Anne sits on a high throne with a rectangular cloth canopy, and between her knees, presumably on a step of the throne, sits the young Virgin with the naked Infant on Her lap. St. Anne is old and wears an old-fashioned wimple; her daughter is very young with long golden hair. Encircling the miniature and text are two branches of a vine-like Tree of Jesse composed of twelve crowned portrait heads of the royal ancestors of Christ set into as many flowers, a seated figure of David playing his harp in a similar flower, and a black lion or dog, possibly the lion of Judah, in the fourteenth flower. At the base of the vine is Jesse, his eyes closed, reclining on a bed.

144. ST. MARY MAGDALENE.  (M – p.294)  Clothed in a houppelande,
[s] long blue cape, and wimple, the Magdalene holds an open jar of ointment and its cover. The black tiles of the floor contain letters from the saint's name. Most of the border consists of orange angels inside the loops of blank scrolls, but at the top is God the Father blessing the Magdalene in the side border, where she is barefoot and dressed simply, as she is often pictured in the wilderness. Along the inner edge of the page is a scroll held by angels and bearing the Latin text of Luke VII, 47, in which Christ explains that many sins are forgiven her because she loved so much.

145. ST. CATHERINE.  (M – p.296)  Oblivious of the spiked wheel and
[s] the reclining executioner with a sword that are on the floor behind her, Catherine reads quietly from an open book. She is portrayed as a princess with a small circlet crown and a long ermine-lined cape. The black tiles of the floor carry designs based on the instruments of her martyrdom. The leaves of the border hold small balls, usually of gold, and a bear cub plays with a red and gold ball. The precise meaning of these motifs is not clear, but they are surely connected somehow with Catherine, who was the patroness of most crafts and trades having to do with wheels and turning machines. The cub (Lat. *catulus*) is probably a pun on her name.

146. ST. BARBARA.  (M – p.298)  Richly dressed, as befits the daughter
[s] of a satrap, she wears a garland or crown with buds in her hair,

and holds her traditional peacock feather. Behind her stands a small tower with three windows at the top, symbolic of the Trinity. The tower motif is used schematically in some of the floor tiles. In the lower border is an animal with long quills or bristles, possibly the porcupine of chastity, but more likely an emblem of Barbara's patronage of a variety of trades having to do with hair or bristles, because of a crude pun on her name.

147. St. agnes. (M – p.300)  As an embodiment of chastity, Agnes is
[s] accompanied by a small lamb, a symbol of purity and a pun upon her name (*agnus* in Latin). She also wears a garland of flowers around her head, and carries a book and a martyr's palm. The border is formed of an elaborate piece of jewelry, probably a necklace, consisting of five engraved gold medallions set with rubies and pearls and joined together by a multi-colored band with several rows of pearls. This object is explained by the legend of Agnes who once preserved her chastity against the advances of a man who sought to tempt her with jewels by claiming to have a fiancé who had already given her "an invaluable bracelet" and a "necklace of precious stones."

148. St. dorothy. (M – p.302)  According to legend, Dorothy promised a doubting pagan scribe on the way to her martyrdom that she
[s] would send him flowers and fruits from Paradise; this story accounts for the garland of flowers in her hair and the golden basket of fruit in her hand. The backdrop is an unusual cherry-colored textile with elaborate patterns in black, gold, and white. Around the page is a bower of gold-leaved vines and gold latticework and, below, the garden of Paradise enclosed by a low brick wall containing two music-making angels and a castellated well or fountain, from which flow two of the rivers of Paradise.

149. St. apollonia. (M – p.304)  Although she has a martyr's palm
[s] and crown, the saint bears only one attribute of her own martyrdom, a tooth held in long iron pincers. In the black floor-tiles dogs are represented crouching and barking, a motif that seems to have no connection with Apollonia.

150. St. agatha. (M – p.306)  Like St. Apollonia, Agatha holds her
[s]  attribute, a severed breast, with iron pincers. She stands against
an intense crimson textile on which is represented a motif in gold
of a phoenix rising in flames toward a burning sun; this motif is
appropriate to Agatha who was known as the fire maiden through
her association with volcanos and lava and her patronage of forg-
ing and casting. Reference to this patronage is to be found in the
border: in her monograms wrought of gold, in the gold and enamel
jewelry, and in gift-wrapped boxes of jewelry. Also in the border
are careful imitations of various kinds of weaving, another craft
of which Agatha was a patroness. A leaf with St. Margaret's portrait
and part of her Suffrage followed this page originally.

151. St. cecilia. (M – p.308)  Lacking all of her normal attributes,
[s]  such as musical instruments, garland, cauldron, and sword, Cecilia
holds a hawk on her gloved hand. She is feeding the bird meat held
on a short stick. The theme of hawking is carried on in the textile
background, which has the repeated motif of a winged boy holding
a white hawk, and in the border of four large feathers charged with
the gold letters C and D (see nos. 116 and 121) linked by chains
from which hang pairs of white wings. These feathers must have
been actual objects, for the little rings and straps by which the
emblems are attached and suspended are rendered in specific detail. Certainly these elements connect Catherine of Cleves to fal-
conry and to Saint Cecilia, but the explanations for this linkage
and for this special iconography of the saint remain to be found.

152. St. lucy. (M – p.310)  Lucy, her neck pierced by the sword of
[s]  her martyrdom, carries the martyr's palm and a book covered in
loose envelope-binding. The border is formed by a necklace or
girdle of silver conch-shaped units to which are attached gold tags
bearing the legend *Luciae Virginis.* The application of the posses-
sive form, "of Lucy the Virgin," is uncertain.

153. St. scholastica. (M–p.313)  Wearing the habit of a Benedictine
[s]  abbess, the order founded by her twin brother with her help,
Scholastica holds a crozier and an open book, probably containing
her rule. The usual attribute of a dove, the form in which she
ascended to heaven after her death, is lacking, but in the border

is an antithetical scene of two boys snaring a bird, though not a dove.

154. St. gertrude. (M – p.315)  In front of a glowing red and gold
[s] textile Gertrude stands reading a book, holding the crozier of an abbess, and dressed in the habit of an Augustinian nun. Because she was a protectress against mice and rats, the pale blue floor tiles show black silhouetted rodents, and the brown tiles have schematic representations of mouse-traps. In the lower border is a scene, set within a fenced garden, of a demon rousing a musing or sleeping peddler whose pack of gold he has just stolen. In back of the peddler are his staff and shield, the latter decorated with a minute image of a woman, probably St. Gertrude, who was the protectress of travellers.

155. St. martha, sister of lazarus. (M – p.316)  The "hostess of
[s] the Saviour" is represented as a housewife or kitchen-maid with an apron, pot of steaming soup, and ladle. Letters, written in capitals, decorate the black tiles of the floor, but they seem merely ornamental in purpose. The spinning female saint in the border seems also to be Martha, for she wears an apron, and her bundle of wool is marked by the letter M, although she is dressed in different clothes.

156. St. helena. (M – p.318)  Portrayed as an older woman with a
[s] wimple, the mother of Constantine wears a gold crown; she holds a book and the cross which was found and recognized by her almost three centuries after the Crucifixion. The reddish purple textile behind her is decorated in gold by motifs of crossed whips of the Flagellation and of crowns of thorns encircling the abbreviated name of Jesus.

157. St. elizabeth. (M – p.321)  As the embodiment of charity,
[s] Elizabeth is surrounded by three beggars; she assists one of them, a crippled man, to put on a shirt that she has just given him. The other two reach up toward her, one with an open hand and the other with a begging bowl. As a gesture of humility she has removed her crown, but she is dressed in expensive, though simple clothes, rather than in the humble Franciscan habit she often wears.

[ 71 ]

# APPENDICES

# APPENDIX A

## Format and Contents of Separate Volumes

GUENNOL VOLUME: Guennol Collection, New York. 193 leaves (present foliation in upper corners ends on fol. 192, because one leaf between fols. 51 and 52 is unnumbered; also an earlier pagination in lower corners, which postdates the division of the manuscript). Leaves are 7⁹⁄₁₆ x 5⅛ inches (192 x 130 mm.); text area is 4³⁄₁₆ x 2⁷⁄₁₆ inches (105 x 62 mm.). 20 lines per page. 27 gatherings, normally of 8 leaves; often with catchwords, all of which appear to be by the same hand, but not by the scribe. Some notes in black ink in the gutters, most of which are directions for the rubricator. Latin texts, whole or part: Hours of the Virgin, Hours of the Cross, Sunday Hours and Mass of the Trinity, Monday Hours of the Dead, Tuesday Mass of the Holy Ghost, Wednesday Hours and Mass of All Saints, Thursday Hours and Mass of the Sacrament, Penitential Psalms, and Office of the Dead. 63 miniatures, 15 large (about 6 x 4¼ inches with borders) and 48 small (2⅜ x 2½ inches without borders), listed by numbers used in the Descriptions of the Miniatures, which is also their order in the Guennol volume: 1–3, 5–13, 15, 17–19, 21–40, 42–48, 60–61, 63–67, 69–78, 98–100. Most text pages decorated with illuminated and penwork initials, with simple illuminated or penwork line-endings, with penwork flourishes and occasional drawings, and with a border decoration consisting of a vertical illuminated bar in the left margin from which a leaf extends horizontally in the upper and lower margins.

MORGAN VOLUME: M.917, Pierpont Morgan Library, New York. 164 leaves (numbered 1–327, odd numbers only, in present pagination in lower right corner of each recto; an earlier pagination in upper right was made after the initial division of the manuscript, but while the Guennol portion was still available, and before the final inclusion of three leaves from the Hours of All Saints [pp. 39–44] and of four text-less leaves with large miniatures [pp. 38, 120, 144, 180; nos. 20, 16, 4, 41]). Measurements and number of lines are identical with Guennol. 28 gatherings, varying from 2 to 8+1 leaves; often with catchwords, all by the same hand as Guennol, except those on p.172 which appear to be by the scribe. Same notes in gutter as Guennol. Two lines of Dutch (pp. 38 and 75), otherwise Latin texts: calendar, Mass of the Dead, Tuesday Hours of the Holy Ghost, Wednesday Hours of All Saints, Friday Hours of the Compassion of God and Mass of the Cross, Saturday Hours and Mass of the Virgin, Office of the Dead, and Suffrages. 94 miniatures, 10 large and 84 small (same measurements as Guennol), listed here by numbers used in the Descriptions of the Miniatures, but arranged according to their order in the Morgan volume: 49–50, 20, 62, 68, 51–54, 56–59, 55, 79–86, 16, 87–89, 4, 91, 90, 92–94, 14, 95–97, 41, 101–157. Decoration of text pages as in Guennol.

[ 75 ]

# Detailed Reconstruction of Manuscript

| ORIGINAL GATHERING | NO. OF LEAVES ORIGINALLY | VOLUME | PAGE OR FOLIO NUMBERS [-1] = Leaf now missing* | TEXT H = Hours, Ms = Mass, O = Office, M = Matins, L = Lauds, P = Prime, T = Terce, S = Sext, N = None, V = Vespers, C = Compline | MINIATURES Nos. in Descriptions of Miniatures H = Hypothetical missing miniature* |
|---|---|---|---|---|---|
| I | 6 | M | pp.1–10 [–1] | two blanks (first missing), calendar | |
| II | 8 | M | pp.11–26 | calendar | |
| III | 8+1 | G | ff.1–9 | H–Virgin (M) | 1–2 |
| IV | 8+1 | G | ff.10–17 [–1] | H–Virgin (M,L) | H,3 |
| V | 8+1 | G | ff.18–25 | H–Virgin (L,P,T) | 4–7 |
| | | M | pp.143–4 | | |
| VI | 8 | G | ff.26–33 | H–Virgin (T,S,N) | 8–11 |
| VII | 8+1 | G | ff.34–41 | H–Virgin (N,V) | 12–14 |
| | | M | pp.155–6 | | |
| VIII | 8+1 | G | ff.42–9 | H–Virgin (C). H–Cross (M) | 15–17 |
| | | M | pp.119–20 | | |
| IX | 8 | G | ff.50–6,(51bis) | H–Cross (M,L) | 18–19 |
| X | 8+2 | G | ff.57–65 | H–Cross (L,P,T,S) | 20–25 |
| | | M | pp.37–8 | | |
| XI | 8 | G | ff.66–73 | H–Cross (N,V) | 26–30 |
| XII | 8 | G | ff.74–81 | H–Cross (C). H–Trinity (M,P) | 31–34 |
| XIII | 8 | G | ff.82–9 | H–Trinity (T,S,N,V,C) | 35–39 |
| XIV | 8+2 | G | ff.90–7 [–1] | Ms–Trinity. H–Dead (M) | H,40–42 |
| | | M | pp.179–80 | | |
| XV | 8 | G | ff.98–105 | H–Dead (M,P,T,S,N,V) | 43–47 |
| XVI | 8+1 | G | ff.106–8 | H–Dead (V,C). Ms–Dead | 48–50 |
| | | M | pp.27–34,45–8 | | |
| XVII | 8 | M | pp.49–60, 35–6,73–4 | Ms–Dead. H–Holy Ghost (M,P,T,S) | 51–55 |
| XVIII | 8 | M | pp.61–72 | H–Holy Ghost (S,N,V,C) | 56–60 |
| | | G | ff.109–10 | Ms–Holy Ghost | |
| XIX | 8 | G | ff.111–6 | Ms–Holy Ghost | 61–63 |
| | | M | pp.39–42 | H–All Sts. (M,P,) | |
| XX | 8 | G | ff.117–23 | H–All Sts. (P,T,S,N,V,C) | 64–68 |
| | | M | pp.43–4 | | |
| XXI | 8+2 | G | ff.124–31 [–2] | Ms–All Sts. H–Sacrament (M) | H,69,H,70 |
| XXII | 8 | G | ff.132–9 | H–Sacrament (M,P,T,S,N,V) | 71–75 |
| XXIII | 8 | G | ff.140–7 | H–Sacrament (V,C). Ms–Sacrament | 76–78 |
| XXIV | 8+1 | G | ff.148–50 [–1] | Ms–Sacrament. H–Compassion (M) | H,79 |
| | | M | pp.75–84 | | |
| XXV | 8 | M | pp.85–100 | H–Compassion (L,P,T) | 80–82 |
| XXVI | 8 | M | pp.101–16 | H–Compassion (S,N,V,C) | 83–86 |
| XXVII | 8+2 | M | pp.117–34 [–1] | H–Compassion (C). Ms–Cross | H,87 |
| XXVIII | 8+1 | M | pp.135–42, 145–54 | Ms–Cross. Sat–H–Virgin (M,P,T,S,N,V) | 88–94 |
| XXIX | 8 | M | pp.157–72 | Sat–H–Virgin (V,C). Sat–Ms–Virgin | 95–97 |
| XXX | 3 | M | pp.173–8 | Sat–Ms–Virgin | |

| | | | | | |
|---|---|---|---|---|---|
| XXXI | 8 +1 | G | ff.151–8 [–1] | Penitential Pss. | H,98 |
| XXXII | 8 | G | ff.159–66 | Penitential Pss. | |
| XXXIII | 8 +1 | G | ff.167–75 | Penitential Pss. O–Dead | 99–100 |
| XXXIV | 8 | G | ff.176–83 | O–Dead | |
| XXXV | 8 | G | ff.184–91 | O–Dead | |
| XXXVI | 8 | G | f.192 | O–Dead | |
| | | M | pp.181–94 | | |
| XXXVII | 8 | M | pp.195–210 | O–Dead. Suffrages | 101–104 |
| XXXVIII | 8 | M | pp.211–26 | Suffrages | 105–111 |
| XXXIX | 8 | M | pp.227–42 | Suffrages | 112–118 |
| XL | 8 | M | pp.243–56 [–1] | Suffrages | 119–124,H |
| XLI | 8 | M | pp.257–72 | Suffrages | 125–132 |
| XLII | 8 | M | pp.273–86 [–1] | Suffrages | 133–139 |
| XLIII | 8 | M | pp.287–302 | Suffrages | 140–148 |
| XLIV | 8 | M | pp.303–16 [–1] | Suffrages | 149–150,H, 151–155 |
| XLV | 6 +1 | M | pp.317–28 [–1] | Suffrages, blank | 156–157 |

\* Of the twelve leaves listed as now missing, one was blank; seven are conjectural leaves with one blank page and one full-page miniature, whose existence is predicated on the consistency of the program of illustration; four leaves are certainly missing from the Suffrages, as is indicated by the gatherings and by the missing texts between M pp. 256–7, 286–7, 306–7, and 316–7; the first and third of these four leaves must have had portraits of Sts. Quirinus and Margaret.

# APPENDIX C

## Calendar

The feasts are transcribed as they appear in the calendar, except that abbreviated words are spelled out, and letters i and j, u and v are normalized. Ordinary feasts in the calendar were written in black, and red was used for major feasts, which are here printed in small capitals; there are no other distinctions of grading in the calendar. In this transcription the golden numbers, dominical letters, and notes on the solar and lunar months are omitted.

### JANUARY

1. CIRCUMCISIO DOMINI
2. Octava Sancti Stephani
3. Octava Sancti Johannis
4. Octava Sanctorum Innocentum
5. Vigilia
6. EPYPHANIA DOMINI
7. Ysidori martiris
8. Eugenii episcopi et martiris
9. Juliani martiris
10. Pauli primi hermite
11.
12. Johannis pape
13. Octava Epyphanie
14. PONCIANI MARTIRIS
15.
16. Marcelli pape
17. Anthonii abbatis
18. Prisce virginis
19. Marii et marthe
20. Fabiani et Sebastiani
21. AGNETIS VIRGINIS
22.
23. Emerentiane virginis
24. Tymothei apostoli
25. CONVERSIO PAULI
26. Policarpi martiris
27. Johannis crisostomi
28. Octava Agnetis
29. Valerii episcopi
30. Aldegundis virginis
31. Ignatii episcopi

### FEBRUARY

1. Brigide virginis
2. PURIFICATIO BEATE MARIE
3. Blasii episcopi
4.
5. Agathe virginis et martiris
6. Amandi et Vedasti
7.
8. Helene virginis
9. Appollonie virginis
10. Scolastice virginis
11.
12. Dorothee virginis
13.
14. Valentini martiris
15. Faustine virginis
16. Juliane virginis
17.
18. Symeonis confessoris
19. Gabini pape
20. Eucharii episcopi
21.
22. CATHEDRA SANCTI PETRI
23. Vigilia
24. MATHIE APOSTOLI
25.
26. Alexandri episcopi
27.
28. Romani episcopi

### MARCH

1. Albini episcopi et confessoris
2. Lucii episcopi
3.
4. David confessoris
5. Foce martiris
6.
7. Perpetue et Felicitatis
8.
9.
10. Clodonii Abbatis
11. Gorgonii martiris

12. Gregorii pape et confessoris
13. Leonis pape et confessoris
14. Innocentius papa
15. Longini martiris
16. Hylarii episcopi et confessoris
17. GERTRUDIS VIRGINIS
18.
19. Johannis heremite
20.
21. Benedicti abbatis
22.
23.
24.
25. ANNUNCIATIO MARIE
26.
27. RESURRECTIO DOMINICA
28. Guntrami regis
29. Gregorii pape
30. Domicii episcopi
31. Sabine virginis

### APRIL

1. Walrici episcopi
2. Nychasii episcopi
3.
4. Ambrosii episcopi
5. Claudiani confessoris
6.
7.
8. Celestini pape
9. Marie egypciace
10. Appollonii presbiteri
11. Leonis pape et confessoris
12.
13. Eufemie virginis
14. Tyburcii et Valeriani
15. Helene regine
16. Kalixti pape
17. Petri confessoris
18.
19. Anthonii martiris
20.
21.
22. Gay pape
23. Georgii martiris
24. Sydrac. Misaac. Abdenago
25. Marci ewangeliste
26. Cleti pape et martiris
27. Anastasii pape
28. Vitalis martiris
29. Petri mediolanum
30. Sophie virginis

### MAY

1. PHILIPPI ET JACOBI APOSTOLORUM
2. Athanasii episcopi
3. INVENTIO SANCTE CRUCIS
4.
5.
6. Johannis ante portam latinam
7. Juvenalis martiris
8. Wyrronis episcopi et confessoris
9. Gengulfi martiris
10. Gordiani et Epymachi
11.
12. PANCRATII MARTIRIS
13. SERVACII EPISCOPI
14.
15. Ysidori martiris
16. Peregrini episcopi et confessoris
17.
18.
19. Potentiane virginis
20.
21. Valerii episcopi
22.
23.
24.
25. Urbani pape
26.
27. Bede presbiteri
28.
29. Maximini episcopi
30. Felicis pape
31. Petronille virginis

### JUNE

1. Nychomedis martiris
2. Marcellini et petri
3. Erasmi episcopi et martiris
4.
5. BONIFACII EPISCOPI
6.
7.
8. Medardi episcopi
9. Primi et Feliciani
10.
11. Barnabe apostoli
12. ODULFI CONFESSORIS. Cunera.
13.
14. Valerii episcopi
15. Viti et modesti
16. Aurei et iustine
17.
18.

19. Gervasii et Prothasii
20. Regine virginis
21.
22. Decem milium martirum
23. Vigilia
24. NATIVITAS JOHANNIS BAPTISTE
25. LEBUINI CONFESSORIS
26. Johannis et pauli
27. Septem dormientium
28. Vigilia
29. PASSIO PETRI ET PAULI
30. Commemoratio pauli

### JULY

1. Octava Sancti Johannis baptiste
2. VISITATIO MARIE. Processus
3. Translatio Sancti Thome
4. TRANSLATIO MARTINI
5. Nychomedis martiris
6. Octava Petri et Pauli
7.
8. Translatio Barbare
9. Octava Visitationis
10. Septem fratrum martirum
11. Translatio Benedicti
12.
13. Margarete virginis
14.
15. Divisio apostolorum
16. Hylarii episcopi
17. Alexis confessoris
18. Frederici episcopi et martiris
19.
20.
21. Praxedis virginis
22. MARIE MAGDALENE
23. Appollinaris martiris
24. Cristine virginis. Vigilia.
25. JACOBI APOSTOLI. Cristofel.
26. Jacincti martiris
27.
28. Panthaleonis martiris
29.
30. Abdon et Sennes
31. Germani episcopi et confessoris

### AUGUST

1. AD VINCULA SANCTI PETRI
2. Stephani pape et martiris
3. Inventio Sancti Stephani
4. Justini presbiteri
5. Marie Ad nives

6. Sixti pape et martiris
7. Transfiguratio christi
8.
9. Vigilia
10. LAURENTII MARTIRIS
11. Tyburcii martyris
12.
13. Ypoliti martiris
14. Vigilia
15. ASSUMPTIO MARIE VIRGINIS
16. Arnulfi confessoris
17. Octava Sancti Laurentii
18. Agapiti martiris
19.
20. Bernardi Abbatis
21.
22. Octava Assumptionis
23. Vigilia
24. BARTHOLOMEI APOSTOLI
25. Gregorii episcopi Traiectensis
26.
27. Rufi martiris
28. Augustini episcopi
29. DECOLLATIO JOHANNIS BAPTISTE
30. Felicis et Adaucti
31. Paulini episcopi

### SEPTEMBER

1. Egidii Abbatis
2. Translatio Agnetis
3. Remacli martiris
4. Marcelli martiris
5. NATIVITAS MARIE
6. Magni confessoris
7. Evorcii episcopi et confessoris
8.
9. Gorgonii martiris
10. Othgeri confessoris
11. Prothi et Jacincti
12.
13.
14. EXALTATIO SANCTE CRUCIS
15. Nychomedis martiris
16. Eufemie virginis
17. LAMBERTI EPISCOPI
18. Columbani confessoris
19.
20. Dyonisii episcopi. Vigilia.
21. MATHEI APOSTOLI ET EWANGELISTE
22. MAURICII ET SOCIORUM EIUS
23. Tecle virginis
24. Conceptio Johannis baptiste

25.
26.
27. Cosme et Damiani
28.
29. MICHAELIS ARCHANGELI
30. Jheronimi presbiteri

## OCTOBER

 1. REMIGII ET BAVONIS
 2. Leodegarii episcopi
 3. Duorum ewaldorum
 4. Francisci confessoris
 5. Appollinaris episcopi
 6.
 7. Marci pape
 8.
 9. Dyonisii cum sociis tuis
10. GEREONIS ET VICTORIS
11.
12. Felicis presbiteri
13.
14. Kalixti pape
15.
16. Galli confessoris
17. Elyfii martiris
18. Luce ewangeliste
19.
20. Quirini martiris
21. Undena milia virginum
22. Severi episcopi
23. Severini Archiepiscopi
24.
25. Crispini et crispiniani
26.
27. Vigilia
28. SYMONIS ET JUDE
29.
30.
31. Vigilia

## NOVEMBER

 1. FESTIVITAS OMNIUM SANCTORUM
 2. COMMEMORATIO ANIMARUM
 3. Huberti episcopi
 4. Modeste virginis
 5. Felicis presbiteri
 6. Leonardi Abbatis
 7. WILLIBRORDI EPISCOPI
 8. Quatuor coronatorum
 9. Theodori martiris
10. Martini pape
11. MARTINI EPISCOPI

12. LEBUINI CONFESSORIS
13. Brictii episcopi
14.
15.
16. Othmari episcopi et confessoris
17.
18. Octava Sancti Martini
19. Elyzabeth vidue
20.
21. Mauricii Abbatis
22. Cecilie virginis
23. Clementis pape
24. Crisogoni martiris
25. KATHERINE VIRGINIS
26. Lini pape
27. Vitalis martiris
28.
29. Vigilia
30. ANDREE APOSTOLI

## DECEMBER

 1. Eligii episcopi et confessoris
 2. Veri et Severi fratrum
 3.
 4. Barbare virginis
 5.
 6. NYCHOLAI EPISCOPI
 7. Octava Sancti Andree
 8. CONCEPTIO MARIE VIRGINIS
 9.
10.
11. Damasi pape
12.
13. Lucie virginis
14. Nychasii episcopi
15. Maximini episcopi
16. Valentini episcopi confessoris
17. Ignatii episcopi
18.
19.
20. Vigilia
21. THOME APOSTOLI
22. Dydimi martiris
23. Victorie virginis
24. Vigilia
25. NATIVITAS DOMINI
26. STEPHANI PROTHOMARTIRIS
27. JOHANNIS APOSTOLI ET EWANGELISTE
28. SANCTORUM INNOCENTIUM MARTIRUM
29. Thome cantuariensis
30. David regis
31. Silvestri pape

# Litany. "Letania Maior"

Only the lists of saints, beginning with the Apostles, are transcribed here. The names are spelled as in the manuscript, except that the letters i and j, u and v are normalized.

Petre
Paule
Andrea
Jacobe
Johannes
Thoma
Jacobe
Philippe
Bartholomee
Mathee
Symon
Thadee
Mathia
Barnaba
Luca
Marce
Omnes sancti apostoli
    et ewangeliste
Omnes sancti discipuli
    domini
Omnes sancti innocentes
Stephane
Line
Clete
Clemens
Sixte
Corneli
Cypriane
Laurenti
Vincenti

Crisogone
Johannes
Paule
Cosma
Damiane
Ignati
Alexander
Marcelline
Petre
Fabiane
Sebastiane
Ponciane
Lamberte
Dyonisi cum sociis tuis
Bonifati cum sociis tuis
Mauriti cum sociis tuis
Gereon cum sociis tuis
Omnes sancti martires
Augustine
Martine
Silvester
Leo
Gregori
Ambrosi
Jheronime
Nicholae
Remigi
Hylari
Servati
Willibrorde

Benedicte
Egidi
Bernarde
Francisce
Dominice
Anthoni
Odulphe
Lebuine
Omnes sancti confessores
Maria Magdalena
Felicitas
Perpetua
Agatha
Lucia
Agnes
Cecilia
Anastasia
Scolastica
Walburga
Ghertrudis
Margareta
Katherina
Barbara
Ursula cum sodalibus tuis
Elyzabeth
Omnes sancte virgines vidue
    et continentes
Omnes sancti

## APPENDIX D

### Selective Bibliography

As the word "selective" indicates, this bibliography is not complete. Instead, it includes only the most prominent works on the Guennol volume and the Cleves Master.

S. Beissel, "Un Livre d'Heures appartenant à S. A. le duc d'Arenberg à Bruxelles: Étude iconographique," *Revue de l'art chrétien,* ser. 4, vol. XV (1904), pp. 437–47.

A. W. Byvanck, *La miniature dans les Pays-Bas Septentrionaux* (Paris, 1937), pp. 65–70, 117–8, 141, 142–3, 145, 146, 149–50, 160; figs. 130–52.

A. W. Byvanck and G. J. Hoogewerff, *La miniature hollandaise* (The Hague, 1922–1926), pp. xxii, 12–3, 21–4, 28–9; figs. 40–48, 55; pls. 25–7, 63–4, 85–90, 110–1, 184, 205–6.

F. Gorissen, "Historische-heraldische Betrachtungen über ein Stundenbuch der Katharina von Kleve, Herzogin von Geldern," *Gelre: Bijdragen en Mededelingen,* LVII (1958), 201–18, 2 figs.

G. J. Hoogewerff, *De Noord-Nederlandsche Schilderkunst,* I (The Hague, 1936), 447–71, figs.

E. Panofsky, *Early Netherlandish Painting* (Cambridge, Mass., 1953), pp. 103ff., 122, 176ff., 242; notes 102[4], 103[7], 118[4]; figs. 128–30.

Rijksmuseum, Amsterdam, *Middeleeuwse Kunst der noordelijke Nederlanden* (Amsterdam, 1958), pp. 19–20, 30, 119–20, 122–127; figs. 83–4.

Kees de Wit, "Das Horarium der Katharina von Kleve als Quelle für die Geschichte der südniederländischen Tafelmalerei und der nordniederländischen Miniaturen," *Jahrbuch der Preuszischen Kunstsammlungen,* LVIII (1937), 114–23, figs.

PLATES

PLATE 3.   Catherine of Cleves Kneeling before the Virgin and Child   [No. 1]

PLATE 4. Annunciation to Joachim [No. 2]

PLATE 5.   Meeting at the Golden Gate   [No. 4]

PLATE 6.  Annunciation to the Virgin   [No. 10]

PLATE 7.   Adoration of the Child   [No. 12]

PLATE 8.  Christ before Caiaphas  [No. 18]

PLATE 9. Flagellation of Christ [No. 22]

PLATE 10.  Christ Carrying the Cross  [No. 24]

PLATE 11. Crucifixion  [No. 26]

PLATE 12.   Descent from the Cross   [No. 28]

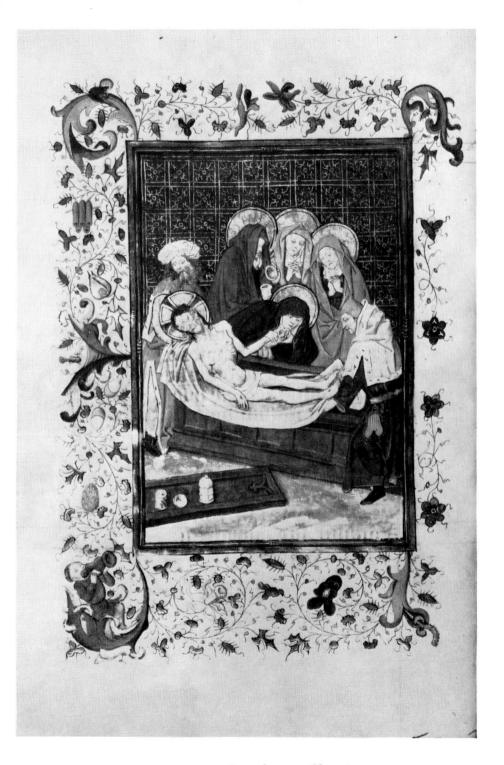

PLATE 13.  Entombment  [No. 30]

PLATE 14. Trinity in an Apse [No. 32]

PLATE 15. Deathbed Scene [No. 41]

PLATE 16.  Pentecost   [No. 51]

PLATE 17. St. Peter Bestowing the Holy Ghost [No. 59]

PLATE 18.  All Saints before God the Father  [No. 61]

PLATE 19.  Solomon Distributing Bread  [No. 70]

PLATE 20.   Last Supper   [No. 77]

PLATE 21.   Queen of Sheba Fording a Stream   [No. 85]

PLATE 22.   Miracles of the Pool of Bethesda   [No. 86]

PLATE 23. Holy Family at Work [No. 92]

PLATE 24.  Crucifix with God the Father, the Virgin, a Bishop Saint,
and Catherine of Cleves   [No. 96]

PLATE 25.   Virgin and Child in a Grape Arbor   [No. 97]

PLATE 26.   Mouth of Hell   [No. 99]

PLATE 27.   St. Philip Apostle   [No. 111]

Anctiffime bartholomee
dei apostole. qui per dec
truchonem ydolozu et
multam operationem miracu
lozum populum no modicu
ad fidem domini nostri thesu
xpisti conuertisti amore. cuius
omnes huius seculi uanitates

PLATE 28. St. Bartholomew Apostle [No. 112]

PLATE 29.   Adoration of the Magi   [No. 116]

PLATE 30.  St. Ambrose   [No. 119]

te fanctus pro lege dei fui
pertauit ufcp ad mortem et
a uerbis impior non timuit.
fundatus enim erat fupra fir
mam petram. V. Corona au
rea fuper caput eius. expreffa
figno fanctitatis glorie horis.
Oremus: Corneli alia an.

PLATE 31. Sts. Cornelius and Cyprian [No. 121]

PLATE 32.  St. Lawrence  [No. 128]

The Trustees and Staff of the Pierpont Morgan Library wish to record their enduring gratitude to the hundreds of Fellows of the Library whose contributions assisted in the acquisition of the Cleves Hours, and especially to the following donors who made major gifts toward this purchase:

OF THIS MONOGRAPH, 1750 COPIES
WERE DESIGNED AND REPRINTED BY THE
HARBOR PRESS, NEW YORK
IN OCTOBER 1964